OF
BRACES
AND
BLESSINGS

OF BRACES AND BLESSINGS

Bonnie Wheeler

CHRISTIAN HERALD BOOKS
Chappaqua, New York 10514

All Scripture quotations in this book are taken from The Living Bible, copyright 1971 by Tyndale House Publishers, Wheaton, Ill. Used by permission.

Library of Congress Cataloging in Publication Data

Wheeler, Bonnie G.
    Of braces and blessings.

    1. Wheeler, Bonnie G. 2. Christian biography—United States.
3.Physically handicapped children—Family relationships. 4. Children, Adopted—Family relationships. I. Title
BR1725.W428A36   280′.4 [B]   80-65431
ISBN 0-915684-63-2

To protect the child, the name of the newest Wheeler is changed in this book; ''Melissa'' is a pseudonym.

MEMBER OF
EVANGELICAL CHRISTIAN
PUBLISHERS ASSOCIATION

Christian Herald, independent, evangelical and interdenominational, is dedicated to publishing wholesome, inspirational and religious books for Christian families. ''The books you can trust.''

First Edition
CHRISTIAN HERALD BOOKS,
40 Overlook Drive, Chappaqua, New York 10514
Printed in the United States of America

Thank You, God...for Dennis

Contents

1
Kaleidoscope

"MRS. WHEELER, I don't want to discourage you, but the adoption picture has undergone many recent changes. We can offer healthy infants only to childless couples, and there's a long waiting list even then. However, there are many children who were previously considered unadoptable, kids that are older, racially mixed, or handicapped. Would you and your husband be interested in one of these children?"

That surprising and edifying conversation did little to dispel the winter gloom of that January 1974 afternoon. I mumbled a vague promise to call the adoption worker again, hung up the telephone, and turned to my husband.

"Dennis, she actually asked if *we'd* consider an older, racially mixed, or handicapped child."

"Bonnie, I know we both want a fourth child, but can we realistically handle *another* child with special problems? Much as we want another child, we have to face facts."

"Facts! Dennis, I know the facts all too well. Our Julie has been wearing leg braces for ten years and determinedly trying to ignore her cerebral palsy. Timmy is a very hyperactive seven-year-old. And Robby, only four, and he already has leg braces and a mouth full of silver teeth. I know the facts. I get to face them every day. Don't we already have enough of specialists, medical bills, hospitals, and complications? How much does God expect us to handle?"

Dennis and I prayed together about the possibility of adoption, then asked each other, and God, "Are 'the facts' God's prevention or His preparation?"

It's now six years and three adopted children later. Eight months after that discouraging phone call, Becky joined our family. She was older *and* racially mixed *and* handicapped. Seven months after that, Benji joined our family. He arrived with an enormous smile and a multitude of medical labels. And three years after Benji, Melissa arrived, a deaf and blind victim of maternal rubella.

I laughingly recall asking Dennis, "How much does God expect us to handle?"

I'm continually amazed at the way God has taken my little faith, my limited wisdom, my puny strength and, like the loaves and fishes, multiplied them beyond my believing.

I rejoice in the way God took our experiences with our first three children and used them to prepare us for the next three.

For a moment, I pause from my reflections and look at my latest needlework project. It's a mess of seemingly random threads.

No symmetry.

Muddy colors.

Nothingness.

I turn the fabric over, and a picture comes into focus:

True-to-life colors.

Beauty.

Symmetry and purpose.

I see the threads of my life in that tangled mess:

Threads that hurt.

Had blurred edges.

Made no sense.

But looking back, I see God, the Master Designer, patiently and lovingly working on me. Preparing me. Stretching my limits. Those loose threads make up the person that I am today, and a kaleidoscope of memories—those loose threads—passes before me:

Playing with children in a local orphanage. Knowing that without my grandparents, I'd be a resident, not a visitor.

The horrid injustices I saw in the South of the fifties, and my childish frustration at my inability to change them.

And there was my best friend. She was my *best* friend. I was her *only* friend. Southern society could forgive her unmarried white mother. Southern society couldn't forgive a seven-year-old child for being fathered by a black man. The other children taunted her about her kinky hair. I just loved her. I had forgotten her until Becky came home crying, "Mommy, David called me 'kinky.'"

On my knees, comforting my black daughter, I was suddenly flooded with memories of long-forgotten experiences with another little girl who had prepared me for this time, this place, this child.

I was fascinated by the story of Helen Keller. Deaf. Blind. For hours, I'd practice "being Helen." I'd stuff cotton in my ears, close my eyes, pretend. Then the game would turn from play to panic, and I'd frantically snatch the cotton from my ears and gratefully open my eyes. My game would end.

And now there's Melissa. Deaf. Blind. But she can't pull the cotton out. For her the game doesn't end. Remembering my moments of childish panic, I hold her tight.

As a lonely child I was an avid reader, and my favorite book was *The Family Nobody Wanted,* a warm story about a couple who adopted many children, loved the Lord, and lived in a big house.

Nobody was lonely *there.*

"When I grow up, that's the kind of life and family I want," I said.

I'd forgotten my childish pledge until a friend gave me a battered old copy, saying, "I thought you might enjoy this."

As I reread that old favorite, I was awestruck at how that vow had been fulfilled. Here we are with our three homemade and three adopted children. Living in a big house. Loving the Lord. And there are very few lonely moments.

Threads that make no sense? Happenstance?

No! Just as I followed a pattern when I stitched these colored threads, so God has a master plan for the tapestry of my life.

I pick up more random threads: the miscarriages that seemed to have no sense or meaning, only pain and loss. Yet out of that pain came the desire for more children. Now three homeless kids have a family, and the pain and sense of loss are gone.

Threads.

Threads that were singed, but never broke.

That hurt, but never broke. Times I saw myself at the edge of a cliff and one more burden, one more snagged thread, would have sent me over the edge. I cried out, *God! God! You promised! No more than I can handle! This is my limit! I'm at my edge!*

And God in His infinite mercy, God the keeper of promises, would let me rest in His arms. Lull me to sleep. Give me a night's rest. In the morning I would awaken, refreshed and strengthened. The limits stretched. The healing started.

The Master Designer had completed another stitch.

2
Julie

AS A LONELY CHILD, raised by my grandparents, I always dreamed of growing up and having children—dream children to fill an empty childhood.

Those children would have all the qualities that I lacked: they would be beautiful (I was plain); golden haired (I was dark); athletic (I was clumsy); and popular (I was extremely shy).

I had all the qualifications for the typical parent who wants her children to fulfill her dreams and fantasies—be all she wanted to be but never was. What a horrible legacy to pass on to our children, an inheritance of empty dreams.

By our second week of marriage, Dennis and I had our future family planned.

"We'll have four children. Two boys and two girls. Then maybe we can adopt one."

The names, conception, and due dates were scheduled and filed. Those four children, each born *exactly* two years after the other, would be perfect. Other people have children with birth defects. Other people are handicapped.

Other people.

That planned, scheduled, and very mythical first child was to be a son and arrive after our third anniversary.

"Mrs. Wheeler, please take these prenatal vitamins," my doctor pleaded.

"No! I won't take anything that can possibly hurt my baby. Haven't you read the papers?"

"Thalidamide Disaster" screamed the newspaper headlines of 1963. There were vivid descriptions of deformed babies, terrified parents, and vows of medical reform. When the publicity first started I panicked. *What if that happens to us?* I thought. Logic soon took over. *As long as I'm cautious and take nothing, our baby will be perfect.*

Eventually I developed anemia and started having fainting spells. Then my doctor insisted, "You take these vitamins before you faint, fall, and injure the baby."

I took the pills, took naps when told, quit work when told, dieted as directed, and prayed. Perfect child guaranteed.

Journal Notes, April 1963

"I recognize the sound of the nurse's rubber-soled shoes as she hurries down the corridor toward my room. She hands me my daughter, then shows me the proper way to hold her.

"Dumb me! I don't even realize there is a *proper* way. 'Hey, Nurse! Don't leave!'

"I'm filled with conflicting emotions: fear, joy, anxiety, curiosity, and utter exhaustion. Mostly, fear.

"'Well, daughter, I guess we'd better get acquainted. I hadn't realized that you'd be so tiny and helpless.' I unfold your pink blanket and take inventory: ten perfect toes, ten perfect fingers, a rosebud mouth, and a dainty face shaped like a miniature valentine. A tiny, beautiful, perfect baby.

"You open your eyes, and for a brief moment you look as scared as I feel. Instinctively, you grasp my finger and snuggle closer.

"'Sleep on, little one. We'll make it. I'm a mother now.'"

"There's something wrong with this baby," nagged Dennis's stepmother. "All my other grandchildren could sit up and crawl long before this." I took her words as a personal criticism and ignored them—or tried to.

I ignored them until I took Julie in for a routine checkup: "Look at her, Doctor! Her feet don't just turn in, they turn backward. It looks like a monstrous joke has been played on her and those frail little legs were put on wrong. Every time she tries to stand and take a step, she trips over her own feet. What's wrong with her?"

He poked and prodded, watched her stand again, then reluctantly admitted, "She does seem to toe in a little. You'd better see an orthopedist."

That first visit with the orthopedist was the beginning of an odyssey filled with pain, frustrations, joys, and braces and blessings. There would be a long series of specialists seeing various parts of our daughter, but never the whole child. There was a pediatrician to treat her illnesses, an orthopedist to check her legs, and a neurologist. ("Mommy, all he ever does is tap me with that little rubber hammer.") As with Humpty Dumpty, no one tried to put all those pieces together.

"She's pigeon-toed. We'll try a night brace," that first orthopedist explained. "It's a fifteen-inch bar attached to the bottoms of her shoes. She'll wear it during naps and at night to train her feet outward. A year, or less, should solve the problem."

We began adjusting to life with braces: only nightgowns, never pajamas with feet; sleepless nights; braces and legs getting caught in crib rails; and other children.

When other kids played with Julie, they would constantly take her toys away, confident that she couldn't catch them. One evening I had bathed her and put her night bar on early. Several neighbors were visiting with their toddlers, and all at once we heard a loud cry.

"Took dolly! I hit!"

Julie had unscrewed the bar from her shoes, crawled over to her tiny tormentor, and whacked him. I gave her a half-hearted scolding and tightened the screws. The kids left her alone.

That evening was the beginning of our determined efforts to let Julie fight her own battles (usually not so literally). We knew that we couldn't always be around to protect Julie, so she would have to learn to stand up for herself. Strangers would see us as cruel, hardhearted, and insensitive. We saw it as very painful and very necessary.

By the time Julie was eighteen months old, I was three months pregnant. We were jubilant and right on schedule. Then shortly after my pregnancy was confirmed, Julie caught German measles. My doctor wasn't too concerned, but he did give me a gamma globulin shot to lessen the chance of any damage to my growing fetus.

In October 1964, I was just starting to show and feeling smug. Then I started to hemorrhage, and smugness and schedules flew out the window.

For weeks I stayed off my feet, made frantic calls to the doctor, and prayed. That autumn, as the falling leaves signified the end of summer dreams, a miscarriage signaled the end of our precious dream and an embryonic life too fragile to survive.

After performing a D & C on me and a biopsy on the fetus, my doctor came to talk with me. He bored me with statistics of miscarriages and then added, ''This is often nature's way of getting rid of a defective baby. Just think of it as something that wasn't meant to be.''

''Was my baby defective? Did the rubella virus hurt it? Was it a boy or girl? What went wrong?'' I begged for answers.

The doctor refused to answer my specific questions and only repeated his stock answers. The word ''defective'' kept haunting me. Had the rubella virus created a damage that God knew I wasn't yet ready to handle?

While I was recuperating, a thoughtful friend gave Julie a puzzle. Unfortunately it was meant for an older child, but that didn't deter Julie. What she lacked in coordination she more than made up for with determination. For over a week, all of Julie's waking hours were spent trying to conquer that puzzle.

"Honey, let Mommy help you."

"No, Mommy, I do it meself!"

One evening Julie triumphantly announced, "I doed it! I doed it all by meself." That same stubbornness and independence that so exasperated me was to save Julie. God had prepared her well.

Julie fell frequently and became adept at administering first aid, Wheeler style. She'd fall, pat the injured part, and tell it, "You OK"; then she'd scurry off until the next time (ten minutes later if we were lucky).

While we lived in our apartment, Julie was usually inside, on the carpet, and seldom got seriously hurt. She celebrated her second birthday in a new house, and while her health improved, her legs seemed worse and she was constantly getting scraped and bruised. By her next appointment with the orthopedist, the poor child was a walking disaster.

"Poor thing," the doctor said. "What happened to her? A car accident?" The doctor was visibly shocked by Julie's appearance. She had three lumps on her head, and her legs were a solid mass of bumps, cuts, and bruises. Julie looked like the sole survivor of a head-on collision. The doctor—finally—believed what I had been telling him about Julie's "clumsiness," and she received her first pair of corrective shoes.

Those next years were filled with frustration and shoes. The doctor tried every possible addition to those shoes. Nothing helped.

"Doctor, these are twenty dollar shoes. We've paid another

twenty dollars for all the extras you've prescribed: cookies, lifts, wedges. Now the shoes are too heavy for her to lift. Her legs turn in worse than before from trying to pick up the extra weight."

He tried again.

"Mommy, all my friends wear neat shoes. They have thongs, sandals, tennies, boots, black shoes, red shoes.... All I ever wear are these white high tops. Everybody calls me a baby. Why can't I wear shoes like the other kids?"

We couldn't afford more than one pair of shoes at a time, and I'd spend Saturday evening trying to cover a week's worth of scratches and scrapes with white shoe polish. I'd spend the rest of the week trying to get that same white shoe polish off the carpet, furniture, and Dennis's dark pants.

"Mommy, everybody's going barefoot. Can I take off my shoes?"

"No, honey. Remember what the doctor said? You have to wear them."

Julie was wearing corrective shoes or braces all but one hour each day (she got an hour off for bath time). Still nothing helped. She looked like a walking accident; her legs still looked backward. We went to a new orthopedist, and a growing fear went with us.

Three months after Julie's third birthday, we presented her with a baby brother. Timmy was her exact opposite—blond, chubby, and by age four months, always on the go.

Julie treated Timmy like a doll for the first months, but once he started moving around she had a few doubts. Timmy got a severe ear infection and cried for two nights, two sleepless nights in which I sat up with Timmy and rocked and rocked.

Julie obviously resented the extra attention this new intruder was getting. "Why does he cry so much, Mommy?"

"His little ears hurt, Julie."

"Can we send him back for some new ears?"

During one unforgettable week in the fall of 1966, Julie and Timmy both had doctor appointments. Timmy's doctor ordered immediate surgery for a small growth on Timmy's tongue. Dennis and I were overly concerned at even minor surgery on one of our precious children. It's a wonder that Timmy didn't get seasick from all my rocking.

Two days later, I took Julie in to see her latest orthopedist. This new doctor was seeing Julie more often and giving her longer exams. But there were still no answers, progress, or improvements. I left Timmy with a babysitter and took Julie in for what I thought was another routine examination.

The exam was even longer and more thorough than usual, and I felt vaguely apprehensive. The vagueness disappeared and the apprehension grew as the doctor led us, for the first time, from the examining room to her private office.

"Sit down, Mrs. Wheeler."

(Uh-oh, that's a bad sign.)

"I don't want you to worry, but—"

(Now I always panic when I hear those words.)

"I'm sure you've wondered why the night brace and corrective shoes haven't helped."

(Oh, God! What is she trying to tell me?)

"I've suspected this for some time now—"

(Dear God, if she's going to destroy me, can't she hurry and get it over with?)

"Julie has cerebral palsy."

Protectively, instinctively, I grasped Julie tighter. Then, mercifully, I blanked out.

I felt no pain.

I cried no tears.

After a time—minutes to the doctor, an eternity to me—she continued. "I'm sure you're picturing telethons with unintelligible spastic kids in wheelchairs. Don't! With CP, the damage is usually done at birth; it's not a degenerative disease.''

I don't know what else was said that day. I was devastated. Numb. Destroyed. *Cerebral palsy.*

We had always been told that Julie's problem would eventually be corrected. "Many kids toe in." "It's temporary."

But cerebral palsy! Those two words were so permanent. So ominous. I was learning that words can often be more crippling than the damage or disability they label.

Somehow, I drove to the babysitter's house to pick up Timmy. While I was there, I called our pastor and asked him to meet me at home.

When I saw the pastor standing by our front door I immediately thought, *Here's comfort. He'll have some answers. Maybe he can pray this numbness away.*

That well-intentioned man walked into the house, took my hands, and with tears of compassion streaming down his face asked, "You poor dear. How long before she dies?"

For the first time that horrid day I was angry with God. *Hey! I don't need this. Enough's enough!*

After I reassured and enlightened the pastor, I called a nurse friend and asked her about cerebral palsy.

"Cerebral palsy is caused by damage to the brain, usually at birth," she said. "Insufficient oxygen is one of the main causes. Fifteen thousand infants are born with CP each year. It's not treated or cured—it's *managed.* A high percentage of CP kids have other involvements: retardation, seizures, vision or speech problems."

Functioning like a robot, I fed Timmy and Julie their lunch and put them both down for naps. I wanted Dennis. I wanted to be held. I wanted to cry. I wanted us to be together. But I also needed answers. That afternoon I read through the information in our encyclopedia and our medical books, and there was no time for tears.

When Dennis finally came home, I gave him the day's mundane news, then unconsciously copied the doctor: "Dennis, sit down, but don't worry...."

Like two shock victims, we walked down the hall to Julie's room. We stood and watched her sleep. I saw Dennis cry for the first time as hand in hand we stood by her bed.

There were the same freckles sprinkled across Julie's button nose. Her flyaway hair was as fine as a freshly woven spider web.

I knew that when she woke up she would *still* be the same cold, cuddly, exasperating, stubborn, lovable, angelic, and mischievous child.

She would *still* have the same pixie face.

She would *still* be the same child who had captured our hearts.

And she would still have cerebral palsy.

For days we wandered around like shell-shocked zombies. I had accepted Jesus as my personal Savior when I was very young; Dennis had no personal relationship with the Lord, but he dealt with the whole situation much better than I did. I still had many lessons to learn on claiming God's promises. Not knowing what else to do, I questioned God:

Why me?

Why us?

Why Julie?

Why?

I had dreamed of this fictional super child, and when I was presented with this child who seemed so different from the dream, I went through an actual mourning process of hurt, loss, and eventual healing.

When I was able to think rationally, I took my questions to the orthopedist.

"Why?"

Patiently, she tried to explain the unexplainable. "Most

CP occurs at birth. I see in your records that Julie was turned wrong. There was probably a slight shortage in her oxygen supply while the doctor was turning her. There was definitely nothing you could have done to prevent this.''

The irony hit me: in spite of all my precautions, something I couldn't control had hurt our child. The one positive aspect of my prenatal overcautiousness was that we avoided the guilt that often debilitates the parents of special children.

While the Wheeler family was struggling through its personal crisis, the war in Viet Nam was raging. Our boys were being chewed up by the machinery of a war no one understood—chewed up, wounded, and mutilated.

The Lord used one of those wounded boys to snap me out of my selfish depression and show me how fortunate we really were.

Jerry was my best friend's brother. He was a strong, sturdy eighteen-year-old boy when he went to Viet Nam. He was a one-legged man when he came home. I visited Jerry with my friend for months after Timmy's birth and Julie's diagnosis. The orthopedic ward that Jerry spent those long months in looked like a picture from Dante's *Inferno*. Fifty beds. All filled. The average age was eighteen. The average loss was two limbs.

Suddenly my precious Julie seemed very strong, healthy, and whole. Through Jerry the Lord helped me get my perspective straightened out and made me finally realize that although she wasn't perfect, *she was perfect for us*.

While her mother was working her way through her traumatic adjustment, Julie continued being the same spunky, determined little girl.

Shortly after her diagnosis, the neighbor children were hanging by their legs from the swing set. Julie's right leg was too weak to hold her weight, and she kept falling. Finally I heard a crash and a loud cry and ran outside.

"Dumb leg! You dumb leg!" Julie yelled. She was sitting on the ground, tears of pain and frustration running down her freckled cheeks. She was beating on the leg. After her outburst, she spent the day trying to swing by her legs. Determined. Spunky. Delightful.

"Hey Julie! Show my cousin how you walk. Guys! Watch this."

Once again, the neighbor kids were taunting Julie. I would usually say a prayer, squeeze my hands together, bite my tongue, and try to let Julie solve the problem. This time I heard music, then laughter. There were ten kids walking like Julie, back and forth, back and forth on the sidewalk. I put Timmy in his playpen and ran outside.

I was greeted by the kids yelling, "Watch our new dance!" Julie piped up, "Mommy, I taught the kids a new dance. They call it 'the Julie.'" She had turned her disability into an asset. And young as they were, those neighbor children became Julie's staunchest defenders and didn't tease her walking style again. Julie wasn't handicapped. She was a choreographer.

One bright summer afternoon, shortly before Timmy's first birthday, Julie and I were "taking baby for a walk." But baby kept walking ahead of us. Timmy would waddle along, then fall on his well-padded bottom; get up, then toddle on.

Julie watched her brother's unsteady progress and turned to me. "I know what's wrong with my legs," she said.

"What, honey?"

"God just musta made me wrong!"

Before I could refute her childish logic, Timmy took another tumble.

Julie looked at the crying Timmy, then looked over at me and said, "Uh-oh! Looks like They goofed on him, too!"

Before Julie started kindergarten, she had a full medical workup: orthopedist, neurologist, pediatrician. We had moved into a new house and were, once again, dealing with new doctors.

The pediatrician declared her healthy and ready for school. The visit with the orthopedist was a shock.

"Mrs. Wheeler," he said, "have you noticed that Julie doesn't use her right hand? [We had, but we just assumed she was *very* left-handed.] Your daughter's involvement includes her entire right side. She *can't* use her right hand, *can't* balance with her right side. Everything on that side is atrophied [smaller]. That leg is even half an inch shorter than the left leg."

Trying to be ever practical, never again emotionally destroyed, I asked, "All right, where do we go from here? Do we start therapy? Are there exercises, surgery, braces? What can we do?"

"There is nothing that can ever help her. No exercises. No therapy. No surgery. To even bring her back again would be a waste of my time and yours."

I could—finally—handle Julie's diagnosis of cerebral palsy.

I could handle the fact that it would always be there.

I could handle that to even partially correct the problem would continue to be a long, slow, frustrating process.

I could *not*—would not—handle just giving up.

How could I look the adult Julie in the eye and tell her that we gave up? We quit? I was so torn. We were told of many doctors, faith healers, diets, and vitamins—even, "I just put Sonny's shoes on the opposite feet, and he got better."

I had seen what great harm—physically, emotionally, and financially—could happen when families spent their lives running from doctor to doctor, state to state, trying to find the answer they wanted. I didn't want that to happen to our family. *Dear God, what do we do now?*

Next on our agenda was a visit with the neurologist. During the exam, punctuated by the doctor's hitting Julie with that ever present little rubber hammer, the doctor warned us of yet another possible problem. "A high percentage of brain-damaged children are also hyperactive." He warned me of symptoms to alert her teachers to.

After the examination he asked, "What therapy is Julie having?" I repeated exactly what the last orthopedist had told me. In all my experience with doctors, they always stick together, and I often wonder if it's part of their Hippocratic Oath. But this doctor was the exception.

"Now look!" he said. "There are many good orthopedists here. You go down this list until you find one who will do something for Julie."

I told the next orthopedist what had preceded our visit, and he solemnly looked me in the eyes. "I can't promise you miracles," he said. "I can't even promise you any major improvements. But I do promise you that we'll do everything possible to help your daughter."

In September 1968, Julie went off to kindergarten, and two-year-old Timmy sadly waved good-bye. That next month, I received so many notes from the school saying, "Julie fell and hit her head today," that I think the school mimeographed copies just for us. I know we set a record in parent-school communication.

The "in thing" during kindergarten was swinging from the monkey bars. Julie couldn't. Her right hand was still too weak to grip the bars, and her left just wasn't strong enough to support her weight. But Julie drew on the same determination she'd used as a toddler to solve a puzzle far too advanced for her, and she made up her mind that she would swing with the other children.

My main memory of that year is of Julie's poor little hands. She tried and tried. She got blisters on her hands. She kept trying and kept falling. More blisters. The kids teased her. The blisters popped and bled. She still kept trying.

Julie was the smallest child in her class. She was still a petite pixie, but with the hardened, calloused hands of a rugged farmer. By spring, Julie came home shouting, "I did it, Mom! I did it! I can swing on the monkey bars, just like the other kids."

After our many notes from school regarding Julie's frequent falls, the doctor decided it was the right time to put Julie into braces full-time.

"Julie, these new braces are called twisters," the orthopedist explained. "They'll support your ankles, turn your feet out, and help your balance. You shouldn't fall so much with this. This is a leather-covered metal waistband. It's connected to cables. The cables run down both legs and attach to your shoes. You'll wear them about twenty-three hours each day. Any questions?"

"What are the kids in my class going to say?" Julie pleaded. "Now they'll really tease me."

To alleviate Julie's apprehensions, I called her teacher, and together we made plans for a special "Show and Tell."

I re-explained to Julie each part of the brace, its function and its name. That morning she wore her favorite dress and matching leotards, and at school the teacher told the class that Julie had something special to show them.

Julie lifted her dress and, starting at the waistband, explained, "These are called twister braces. They're to help my legs turn out. Now I won't fall so much...."

There were many times when Julie triumphed over her limitations, and there were many times when the frustrations almost bogged us down. Dennis was unable to leave work and go on our numerous doctor visits, and it often seemed to be me and Julie against the world. We had no association with other handicapped children, parents, or organizations. Julie thought she was the only child in braces, except for the few she saw on television.

The doctors were excellent, but each was still concerned with treating a part of Julie. No one but me seemed to care about what all this was doing to Julie, the sum of all those variously treated parts.

The one time I called an organization for the handicapped and vented my frustrations, the worker listened patiently and then replied, "It's often harder for a child, like Julie, to adjust and accept her limitations. She appears normal until she attempts something that her limitations prevent or restrict. With a very involved child, it's obvious what the limits are and they seem more accepting." It was interesting information, but it wasn't a solution. There didn't seem to be any.

It was almost impossible to find the proper balance between sympathy and disabling pity. "You never give me any sympathy!" Julie would say. "Why am I like this?" "That new kid stared at me all day!"

"Julie, I know God has a reason for this. I don't know what it is now, but maybe someday we will."

"But Mommy! I want to know now!"

There were many times when Julie would come home with hurts that bandages couldn't help. Not knowing what else to do, she would climb on my lap and we would hug each other tight. I would try to *love* the hurt away.

"We have nothing to fear but fear itself" is an often quoted statement. It originally applied to a war situation, but it can just as easily apply to life with a special child.

We never told Julie "you can't" (she wouldn't have believed us anyway), and she became adept at finding her own limits—and stretching them.

When the neighbor children were learning to ride bikes and roller skate, so was Julie, just a little slower and with a little more effort.

Mothers of special children need healthy egos, and I'm

afraid mine was not always in the best condition. Julie was wearing braces twenty-three hours each day (as prescribed by the doctor), but I took the blame: "It's too hot. Can I take them off?" "I'm sick. Do I have to sleep with them?" "I'm going to a party. Can't I wear pretty shoes?"

After Julie had been wearing the braces for six months, there was a marked improvement, and a cycle started that was to continue into junior high school. The doctor would notice the improvements and tell Julie, "You can try just sleeping in your braces until your next visit."

"Mommy, can I get new shoes? I want sandals, and boots, and buckle shoes, and...."

Two months later we returned, and the doctor sadly told Julie, "I'm sorry, but your legs are starting to turn in again. You'll have to go back to wearing your braces full-time."

Julie, sometimes frustrated, sometimes depressed, was never defeated. She came home from school one day brimming with disgust. "Mommy, what's a cripple? Some dumb boy called me one today. I told him 'I can't be! I don't even know what it means!' "

During her first two years of school, I followed the neurologist's advice and talked with the teachers about the possibility of Julie's having trouble with her attention span and concentration. As long as the work was easy and the time limits were short, there was no problem. But by the second grade she was definitely having trouble.

"Julie's falling behind, yet she tries so hard," the concerned teacher informed me. "She needs help that I can't give her."

We went back to the neurologist, and after another lengthy exam and a battery of lab tests, Julie was started on Ritalin. We explained to Julie that she was like a clock. "You seem fine on the outside, but inside everything is going too fast. That's why you study and work so hard and still have trouble with your schoolwork."

I had read all the dire reports on Ritalin (the drug most commonly used to control hyperactivity), but we trusted the doctor's judgment and were more concerned with Julie's present emotional health than with possible future side effects.

Julie was caught in a web of frustration, and her ego was badly battered and bruised. She loved to read but read so fast that she had little comprehension of what she'd just finished. Her writing was horrid, and math was impossible.

Three weeks after the medication was started, I heard from a jubilant teacher, "There's been an 80 percent improvement in everything. Julie reads better and understands her math. Her handwriting has even improved."

After a series of miscarriages, we were blessed with another boy in November 1969. Robby entered the world with a thick thatch of black hair and a multitude of medical problems. Robby cried almost continually, either from his chronic colic or his monthly ear infections.

In the early months I was often tense and easily upset as I tried to cope—in my own strength—with Julie's needs, the rambunctious Timmy, and a constantly crying baby.

The next few years were a rapidly rising crescendo of problems, but there were triumphs sprinkled along the way:

Julie flashed the smile that always warns me I'm about to be conned. "I want to help the kids that are worse off than me."

"Doing what, Julie?" I asked.

"Well, Mom, if I go on the March of Dimes Walkathon, that would help them."

"Walkathon?" It sounded ominously strenuous, but I heard her out.

"It's twenty miles, and lots of kids are doing it because they want to help the kids that can't walk at all! Can I go? Please, Mommy."

"Twenty miles?" I gulped.

When Dennis came home, Julie tried that effective smile of hers on him. He not only gave his consent but also pledged fifty cents per mile, figuring her weak legs couldn't possibly carry her that far.

Julie had plans to go with some friends, and I asked one of the other mothers, "Could you please have Sandy watch out for Julie and have her call me if there are any problems?"

The day of the walkathon, Dennis and I tried to hide our fears from the confident Julie.

"Bye! Be sure you have my money ready, Daddy!" she shouted as she started out.

I knew the group was due to pass our church, and I "just happened" to be there when the girls came straggling by. Julie was trailing but seemed fine. "Call when you're ready to be picked up!" I urged.

"When we finish, Mom. When we finish."

I waited hours for Julie to call. She had started at nine in the morning, and I had seen her at noon. The call didn't come until after five o'clock. After eight long hours, an exhausted but jubilant little voice said: "We made it, Mom! Come and pick us up. Tell Daddy to have my money ready!"

Four sweaty, sunburned girls piled into the car, all jabbering at once:

"Mom, I got blisters, cramps, sunburn, and am I ever limping!"

"You should have seen Julie. She was beat and we kept telling her to call you, but she wouldn't."

"When we couldn't get her to quit, we all slowed down so she wouldn't be left behind. When we saw that the last few miles were uphill, we all groaned and tried to talk her into calling you. Julie just gritted her teeth and kept walking."

"So I pushed her, Sandy pulled her, Debby tugged...."

Julie spent the next few days in bed. Her overworked muscles had spasms for hours. It was weeks before she could comfortably walk again. But none of it mattered—not the pain, the sunburn, the cramps, the blisters, the spasms, or the exhaustion. Nothing mattered but Julie's personal victory.

"I made it! I really made it!"

3
Timmy

"HI, Cutie. Are these blankets for your new baby?"

"Yes, ma'am," answered three-year-old Julie.

"Is your new baby at home?"

"No, silly! It's still in my mommy's tummy."

I was a more cooperative patient during this pregnancy; I even took my vitamins without a fuss. But when the doctor and I discussed anesthetics, I refused all of them. "If this baby is turned wrong, I'll just have to put up with a longer delivery and let the baby position itself."

Timothy Dennis made his entrance on July 30, 1966. We had a healthy, chubby, blond son, and Julie had a brother. We were all ecstatic.

With Timmy I had rooming-in privileges in the hospital and was able to care for him during the daytime. I loved every minute of it—well, almost every minute. Timmy kept choking on mucus. He'd choke and I'd jump out of bed, ripping a few stitches on the way. I'd grab the suction syringe, and Timmy would be sound asleep with a faint angelic smile on his face, as if to say, "Gotcha!"

"Here's your new baby brother. Now you help your mommy take good care of him." With that introduction from a very wise, thoughtful nurse, Julie met her brother. Joyfully we took our family home.

Those first weeks with two children were exciting and exhausting. Julie was almost three and a half and was used to being an only child. Timmy was a husky nine pounder who wanted to be fed often. I learned that first week that comparisons would never work. Julie came home from the hospital weighing a dainty six and a half pounds, and we tried all the old tricks to keep her interested in her bottle and awake long enough to finish. That was definitely not a problem with Timmy.

Julie was eighteen months old when she walked and started getting into things. By that age she was smart enough to know the meaning of "no" and its consequences. Timmy was crawling, sitting up, and walking around the furniture by six months.

Julie was such an easy child to discipline that by her third birthday we felt well-qualified to write a book on raising the perfect child. Then along came Timmy, and any thoughts of books of parental wisdom rapidly flew out the window.

Julie put a nontoxic crayon in her mouth, hated the taste, and never bit another. Timmy ate crayons by the box.

Julie would see a leaf or cigarette on the ground, take one taste, yell "yuck!" and never sample that thing again. Timmy ate anything that didn't bite back—and a few things that did.

Julie got a mild electrical shock and learned instant respect for electricity. Timmy tried to "fix it" with a hairpin and received third-degree burns on both hands.

By the time Timmy was six months old, we'd given up hope of writing that book and were reading all the books by *real* experts that we could find.

"Doctor, what am I going to do?" I'd say. "He's already into everything and has no idea what 'no' means. What am I going to do?"

The amused doctor replied, "When they start moving around this early and are this active, there's only two things you can do: put away everything you value, and pray you live through it.''

Once Timmy started crawling, we have only blurred photos of him. Dennis would position his son for the perfect picture and plead, uselessly, ''Stay still, Timmy!''

Timmy would smile sweetly, then chase after Daddy. Dennis would rapidly back up, only to be pursued by Timmy. We would go in for well-baby checks, and Timmy would grab the nurses; he would laugh while the doctor checked him; he would flirt while the nurses prepared to give him his shots. He would watch everything closely, grinning all the time. Timmy was in love with the world. He was so happy and smiled and laughed the most of any baby I had ever seen. For a time.

The week that I took Julie to the orthopedist and got the devastating news about her cerebral palsy, we also found out that Timmy would need surgery. ''He has a rapidly growing tumor on his tongue, and it will have to be removed,'' the doctor said. Timmy smiled his way through the lab tests, and when I left him at the hospital the little ingrate even smiled and laughed as he waved good-bye to me.

Dennis and I almost didn't survive. Timmy did just fine. The growth was benign and the surgery uneventful. Timmy cut his first tooth that same week and decided it was safer to start feeding himself than to take a chance on my getting near his stitches or tooth.

It was in the first months after Timmy was born that I visited with my girlfriend at the military hospital where her brother Jerry was a patient. After a few hours in that ward of teenage amputees, I'd come home to see Julie and our strong, sturdy son. During those visits I became convinced that the first pacifist was a mother.

After one visit in which I'd talked with a boy who had lost both arms, I came home and tightly held Timmy. Timmy took his chubby, strong hand and held my finger tight as he fell asleep. I wept for all the mothers who had held their sons like this, only to see them mutilated later. I wrote in Timmy's baby book:

This Hand

This newborn hand tightly holds
my finger.
So soon it will grow to hold:
Sissy's braids,
His favorite toy, my heart.
This hand will throw balls to Dad,
Pull puppy's ears, kitty's tail.
This hand will carry books to school,
Struggle to use pencil and pen,
Fly a kite, bounce a ball.
Hold a girl's hand, release mine.
Drive a car, pack his clothes,
Leave our home.
Caress a woman, hold his child.
But, dear God!
Will this hand then go to war,
Hold a gun, Lord...
Then hold no more?

When I wasn't caring for the children, going to the doctor, or visiting Jerry, we went looking for a bigger home. One Realtor watched eighteen-month-old Timmy running around the office and said, "Have I got the house for you!"

Our new home was at the end of a court. There was a walkway on one side and lots of safe freedom for the two children. There were also seventeen other children on the court.

On our first walk we met our new neighbors. Kevin had spent his first months in the playpen in a big-city apartment. Timmy was walking. Kevin was in a stroller. I can still picture the pristine whiteness of Kevin's outfit.

Kevin had a balloon, and Timmy wanted it. Timmy waited until his new friend was out of the stroller. Then he made his move. Kevin was left sitting in the mud (in his formerly white outfit), and Timmy had the coveted balloon.

We settled into the new house; Julie started school, and Timmy enjoyed having my undivided attention during those hours. When Timmy was almost three and a half, we were blessed with a third child. Timmy had to adjust to less attention as I tried to cope with Robby's constant pain and tears. Timmy was soon to reclaim my attention.

In April 1970, the seventeen children on our block were outside, taking advantage of a beautiful spring day. They were at the end of the court, playing "crack the whip." One of the older boys had Timmy on his shoulders when suddenly he tripped. Timmy fell off his shoulders and hit the back of his head on the asphalt.

I heard Timmy's screams and ran outside. He was lying in the street, surrounded by worried kids. I'd never heard Timmy scream that loudly before, but a quick check disclosed no bumps or bruises. "Come on, Timmy," I said. "Let's rock until your head stops hurting."

An hour later, Dennis came home. I was still rocking, and Timmy was still screaming. There has always been a special magic between Dennis and the children, and no matter how badly hurt they are, they'll stop crying for him. That day Timmy didn't—couldn't.

I called the hospital and was told, "Bring him in immediately." They examined Timmy and x-rayed his head. "No signs of a fracture, no concussion that we can find. If he throws up or acts strange in the next twenty-four hours, bring him back."

Timmy calmed down, stopped crying, and had a good night's sleep. I woke up the next morning to the sound of his retching. We hurried back to the emergency room.

"Timmy has a slight concussion. Keep him quiet for a few days and he should be fine," the doctor reassured.

The tricky part would be keeping the rambunctious Timmy quiet. Somehow we managed for the next few days, and he seemed fine.

A week after Timmy's fall and apparent recovery, I was awakened again by the sound of his retching. By the time I reached his bed, Timmy was asleep again. Then I really got worried.

We'd always joked that Timmy had only two speeds: "fast" and "asleep." There were never any in-between stages. He was never drowsy or tired—until that day.

I cleaned up around Timmy and let him sleep. Twenty minutes later, I heard those sounds again and found him sitting up, trying not to soil his bed. By the time I grabbed a washrag and towel, he was sleeping again. Trying hard not to be alarmed, I called the doctor.

"It's probably just a virus," the doctor said, "but bring him on in."

Frantically, I called my neighbor to watch Julie and a very ill, five-month-old Robby. I was getting more and more frightened. Timmy fell asleep in the car and slept through the drive to the doctor's office. In the examining room I helped Timmy get undressed. He promptly fell asleep on the examining table. I was no longer *just* frightened.

The doctor strode briskly into the room, skidded to a stop, and joked, "He must really be sick. First time I've seen him still."

Timmy woke up, and the doctor watched him walk across the room. As Timmy drunkenly staggered a few feet, the doctor stopped smiling. There were no more jokes. "I'll call ahead. You take him straight to the neurologist."

"Doctor! What's wrong with him?"

"Now, don't worry. It's probably just a virus, but after

that head injury I'd like the neurologist to check Timmy.''

Timmy slept as we drove across town to see the other doctor. My terror grew when I gave our names to the nurse and we were *immediately* taken to the doctor.

After checking reflexes and examining Timmy's eyes, the neurologist turned to me and said, "I want you to take your son directly to our Redwood City Hospital. I'll call ahead and warn admitting that he's on the way.''

"Why Redwood City?''

"That's where we send our neurosurgery cases. I'm afraid Timmy has a blood clot as a result of last week's fall and concussion.''

I was stunned, unbelieving. *This must be a nightmare*, I thought. *I'll go to sleep, and when I wake up this nightmare will be over.* But it wasn't over. It had just begun, and the nightmare would shadow our lives for the next eight years.

Trying to still my mounting terror, I crammed my "sleeping" son into the telephone booth. I was too upset to drive, and I wanted Dennis to come and pick us up. Frantically, I dug through my purse for change.

Dear God, please let me have some money!

(I found one dime.)

"Operator, I want to place a collect call.''

Dear God, please let his secretary accept my call.

(She did.)

Timmy kept slumping over, and I tried desperately to hold him up and hang on to the phone while I explained the problem to Dennis. As we waited for him to arrive, I held my unconscious son tightly and prayed as a litany, *Help him, help him, help….*

Dennis arrived and we made a frantic drive across the bridge to Redwood City. Timmy was still "sleeping," but we both knew it wasn't a natural sleep.

The emergency room crew was ready for us, and after a

quick exam Timmy was admitted to the pediatric neurosurgery ward.

"First, we have some papers for you to sign," we were told. "They're consent forms for brain surgery. If it becomes necessary, we'll try to call you first. But if that clot starts to move, there might not be time to reach you. Please sign here."

I glanced at Dennis and said, "This can't be Timmy. He's always been the strong, sturdy, healthy one. He's always seemed so indestructible."

Whenever I picture hell, it's always a combination of the orthopedic ward at the military hospital and that neurosurgery ward where they took Timmy.

Most of the tiny patients were recovering from brain surgery. *Grotesque* is the kindest word I can use to describe what I saw. (I can't forget it; Dennis can't remember.) The surgery sites caused gross swelling and distorted their poor little heads. The ones who didn't have their entire heads swathed in bulky bandages looked even more bizarre with their stubbly shaved heads.

Oh, dear God! There's been a mistake! I can't leave my son here!

They took Timmy away from me, and Dennis filled out the endless forms. Another mother came over to me. She was carrying her daughter. I could tell it was her daughter by the pink nightgown. Her tiny head had recently been shaved; her face was swollen and bruised; there was a partial bandage on her head. The poor baby was barely recognizable as human, much less as a daughter.

That's what they're going to do to my son!

The mother asked, "What's wrong with your son?"

I explained what little I knew.

"Oh, you're facing the same surgery my daughter just had. I always find it so comforting to talk to other mothers. Don't you?"

My mouth was dry; my hands were shaking; I couldn't answer. Comforted? "Lady, I'm scared to death!" I felt like saying.

They ran tests on Timmy all afternoon: brain scans, skull X rays, an electroencephalogram (EEG). When he returned from the last test, there were dozens of little rivulets of blood mingling in with his golden hair.

"Don't look so upset, mother," the doctor said. "We put little pins in his head for the test. It wasn't as bad as it looks, and he was partially sedated. He won't remember a thing."

Dennis and I stood by Timmy's bed, too frightened to even talk. If we spoke it would have been about Timmy, and those thoughts were too frightening to put into words.

The doctor went on: "Mr. and Mrs. Wheeler, the tests confirm your neurologist's diagnosis. It's unusual for a blood clot to develop from such a slight concussion. And they usually show up sooner than this. Very strange. We'll be running more tests and monitoring him constantly. You two go home and rest while you can."

We both knew there would be no resting.

On the way home I babbled to Dennis, "They'll shave off Timmy's hair. I just know when it grows back it'll be dark stubble, not that beautiful blond silk."

Dennis later told me, "I thought you'd really flipped! We'd just signed papers for brain surgery, and the doctors were certain they'd be opening his skull, cutting into his brain. He could die, and all you talked about was his hair." We eventually realized that my preoccupation with Timmy's hair was a defense mechanism, an escape from reality.

The next morning I got a good look at reality. I got up, fixed Dennis and Julie their breakfast, and got Dennis off to work and Julie off to school. Then I medicated Robby, checked in with his doctor, washed his diapers, fixed the day's supply of formula, took him to my neighbor's, and set off to visit Timmy.

That first day, Timmy floated in and out of consciousness, but once he started being alert and awake for longer periods, he was horribly afraid. He refused to eat, cried constantly, and begged us to take him home. The nurses were monitoring him constantly; he was surrounded by scary-looking children; and he was subjected to painful, frightening tests.

On the sixth day of Timmy's hospitalization, the doctor met me in Timmy's room. "Mrs. Wheeler, for some unknown reason Timmy's blood clot is dissolving on its own," he said. "There's nothing more that we can do for him here that you can't do at home. He's so miserable here. Take him home today. Bring him back next week. Keep him as quiet as possible; he still staggers. And whatever you do, don't let him fall and bump that head."

We went home. Timmy still had his blond hair. He hadn't had the surgery. The clot was dissolving. *Everything will be fine now,* or so I thought.

I vaguely recalled the doctor's saying something about Timmy staggering, but I was so excited about bringing him home that I really didn't hear everything he had told me.

Jubilantly I brought Timmy home and set him down. He wobbled down the hall like a little drunk. *Dear God, how am I going to manage to keep him from bumping his head when he can barely walk?* My excitement at having Timmy home was fading quickly.

"Mommy! Mommy!" The hysterical screams shattered the quiet night air. Heart pounding, I ran into Timmy's room. "Bad dream, Mommy! Bad dream." For the next year that would be our nightly ritual.

Timmy was home. He looked the same, was almost well, hadn't needed the dreaded surgery. But he wasn't the same. The smiling, bubbly, always happy child was gone. We had brought home a frightened, insecure, nightmare-ridden stranger, and throughout the next year we would have to learn to cope with him. This stranger hit his sister, yelled at his baby brother, and cried for no apparent reason.

Timmy seldom talked about the hospital and never mentioned the tests. The nurses had assured me that he'd remember none of the painful tests. The nightmares continued. The next month we returned to the hospital for a final EEG.

Timmy was holding my hand, chattering away as we walked down the corridor. Suddenly he went berserk.

"No! Mommy! No!"

He screamed hysterically, sobbed, and fought me off. As we'd passed through the doors, his half-forgotten memories emerged and he screamed, "That's where they put pins in my head! It bleeds and it hurts! Don't let 'em, Mommy! Don't let 'em!"

Trying to ignore the stares of curious strangers, I attempted unsuccessfully to calm him down. I finally managed to get him into the room where the tests were run. (There was a truck strike that prevented new equipment from arriving. When they run the test now they use painless, paste-on electrodes.) The technician sedated Timmy and made me leave the room. I closed the door and walked down the hallway.

Closed another door.

Raced down yet another corridor.

Closed another door.

I could still hear Timmy screaming my name.

Timmy started kindergarten on schedule and promptly fell in love with his teacher. She was a soft-spoken Oriental, and Timmy made an all-out effort to please her. She left at Christmas to have a baby, and Timmy felt betrayed.

The new teacher arrived. She looked at Timmy. Timmy looked at her. War was declared. "Your son is hyperactive, has perception problems, and needs psychological testing," she bluntly told me.

"Do you think Ritalin would help his hyperactivity?" I asked hopefully.

"Mrs. Wheeler, your son is so slow that even if we could control his hyperactivity, it wouldn't make much difference in his learning."

I came out of that meeting filled with conflicting emotions: furious at her character assassination of a five-year-old; horrified at the prospect of Timmy's scholastic future; and starving for some good, positive part of Timmy that we could work on and encourage.

The part of the brain that Timmy had injured controls visual perception, and the pieces seemed to fit together. That plus Dennis and I having been raised in an era in which teachers were accepted as minor deity had us accept what "the teacher" told us.

Timmy would come home from school, kick the dog, hit his little brother, and yell at me. Then he would go to his room and sob. One evening during dinner, Timmy turned to talk to Daddy. As he turned he knocked over a glass of milk. When he started to pick up the broken glass, Timmy bumped heads with the baby, who promptly started crying.

Before the words to Daddy were out of his mouth, Timmy had spilled his milk, broken the glass, bumped his head, and made the baby cry. Before we had a chance to reassure him, Tim dashed from the table, sobbing, "I'm so dumb. I can't do anything right. I'm so dumb."

I again went to see Timmy's teacher. "Timmy has a very poor self-image," I said. "Do you have any ideas on how we can help him?"

She answered: "Five-year-old boys don't have poor self-images. Possibly he's heard the other kids call him dumb. I'll check on that." (I don't have her college degree or her teaching credentials, but I do know a self-image problem when I see one.)

It was recommended that Timmy go into a transitional class after kindergarten. (That's a class between kindergarten and first grade for children who need the extra year.)

Dennis and I had a meeting with the transitional teacher to arrange some testing for Timmy. "He's a cute, lovable child," she said, "and there doesn't seem to be any perception problem. I do feel that he's had about all the failure and stress he can handle. I'm going to test him and find out what he *can* do well. If I discover that the only thing he can do well is draw yellow circles, then that's all I'll have him do. When Timmy's convinced that he's the best yellow-circle drawer in the class, then—and only then—I'll get him to try a red square."

At last! Something positive to work on. (Since that conference, I've often used that method for building up little egos. Everyone has *at least* one area he can excel in, even if it's just drawing yellow circles.) That positive and encouraging conversation with a wise and caring teacher was the calm before the storm.

Smash!

"Mommy, help me!"

Timmy came running into the house with his hand over his mouth and his screams piercing the air. When he took away his hand, blood gushed out. For one crazy moment I thought his mouth had been replaced by an overripe eggplant—a very purple, very bloody eggplant. Tim's lips and gums were a mangled, bloody mess. Two teeth were dangling, but his poor mouth was too much of a mess for me to extract them.

Timmy and his friend had been throwing rocks, and Timmy's mouth got in the way. We made a hurried trip to the dentist, and Timmy was restricted to liquids for the rest of the week.

Timmy celebrated his first day back on "real" food by riding downhill on a go-cart. Unfortunately, it was a go-cart without brakes. Tim used his face. He bruised the bruises; lost another tooth; more liquids.

"Son, please stay in the backyard for a few days. Your poor mouth needs a chance to heal, my nerves need a rest, and the doctor bill needs a break. Anyway, it's safer in the backyard, and maybe you can keep your remaining teeth for a while."

Timmy quickly got bored with his captivity. For entertainment, he stuck his finger through a knothole in the fence. Meanwhile, the neighbor's dog, guarding the other side of that fence, decided to investigate this strange object invading its territory.

Our pediatrician shook his head while he disinfected Timmy's bitten-to-the-bone finger. He applied thick bandages to the wound, gave him a tetanus shot, and started him on Ritalin.

I took Timmy on to school—maybe he'd be safe there!—mangled mouth, missing teeth, bandaged hand, and swollen arm (his immediate reaction to the tetanus shot). The teacher took one look at Timmy, the walking accident, gave him a big hug—carefully—and turned to me and said, "You poor thing. Go home and rest while you can."

We were well aware of the bad publicity that Ritalin was getting in the press; "Teachers Drug Kids" seemed to be the favorite headline in 1972. We found the exact opposite to be true. Timmy's and Julie's teachers bent over backward to avoid any hint that they were recommending the drug. Once again we saw it as a godsend.

Ritalin didn't become Timmy's "smart pills," but it did help him cope better with school, and school with him. I often came out of teacher conferences feeling like a drug pusher, but I thought my ego could handle the battering better than Timmy's.

The average school, neighborhood, home, and mother's nerves are not equipped to handle children who always run at high speed, never walk, and never talk when they can yell.

At night I'd go into Timmy's room to listen to his prayers.

Exhaustedly, I'd drop onto his bed. "Mommy, I'm always so bad," he'd say. And then he'd say his prayers: "Dear God, please forgive me for being such a bad boy. I'm sorry. Amen."

After prayers I would stay to talk. "Honey, you weren't bad today—uh, just a little too loud and active. But you weren't bad."

"But I musta been bad, Mommy. Everyone's always yelling at me!" Then it would be my turn to ask forgiveness—from God and my son.

The Ritalin helped during school hours, but we tried to avoid using it after school and on weekends. During those years there were never any complete answers. No positive cures. No solutions. Painfully we muddled through each day.

We'd always tried to never make Julie and Robby (who by now was also in leg braces) feel handicapped. We always assured them that they were "special." When I got Timmy's pills, I sat down and explained to him, "These are to help you slow down. We know you try your best and it's not always your fault. These will help."

Timmy looked at me with those huge eyes and asked quietly, "Will these be my very own? No one else's? Just mine?"

"Yes," I said, "these will be just your pills."

Timmy broke into a big grin. "Oh goody! This must mean I'm special too!"

When our pediatrician put Tim on Ritalin, he sent in a request to the school district for Tim to be tested. For a year we kept getting postponed. "Timmy's coping," school officials said. "We can only test those kids that can't cope." Meanwhile, we were told of memorization trouble and letter reversals. But they'd always say, "He's coping."

Then one day, "Mrs. Wheeler? This is Doctor X, and I'm the district psychologist."

"Terrific! We've waited a long time for this."

She sounded puzzled but continued, "We want to test your son for our mentally gifted program."

Much to her consternation I started laughing. After all the waiting, all the conferences and complaints, and all Tim's problems, they wanted to test him for the gifted program!

I apologized for my laughter: "I'm sorry, but we've tried to get Tim tested, but not for this program. There must be some mistake."

"Mrs. Wheeler, let me assure you, we don't make that kind of mistake. Tim scored very high on some state tests, and as a result of those high scores I'm to test him."

Poor lady. She was so used to mothers trying to convince her "My child is a genius!" that she didn't know how to handle me.

Timmy did well on the tests, scoring considerably above average, but not quite well enough to qualify for that program. We were thrilled anyway. We tried to pass on our excitement to Timmy. "Think how much improving you've done to even be tested for the program!" we said. "And this has to prove to you that you're not dumb. Definitely not!"

Timmy's behavior was improving, but he still had trouble with acting, and reacting, too fast. He often acted faster than he could think, and sometimes the results were painful.

"Betcha can't catch me!"

Smash! Smash!

Timmy and Robby were playing chase, and Robby darted in the front door and locked it. Tim automatically put his hand through the glass to unlock the door. He got a very deep cut that just missed the main artery. (I rather imagine Timmy has gone through a long succession of guardian angels. The poor things probably asked for early retirement.)

The boys' evening prayers were classic in passing the blame. Robby prayed, "Dear God, help Timmy's cut get well, and *forgive him* for putting his hand through the glass."

Timmy darted a quick glance at his little brother, bowed his head and prayed, "Dear God, please help my cut get better, and *forgive* Robby for locking that door."

My prayer was much briefer: *Dear God, help!*

4
Robby

"YIPPEE! We're gonna have a baby!" Julie and Timmy shouted with excitement when Dennis and I told them of our expected baby. Then in August of 1968 I miscarried. We waited a few months as prescribed by the doctor, and by Thanksgiving I knew I was pregnant again.

And again I miscarried.

Once more we were told to use precautions for a few months. And we did. Honest! But in February, when I went in for my six weeks checkup after the last miscarriage, I was pregnant again.

I had a new obstetrician, and he immediately put me on a salt free, low calorie diet; restricted my activities; gave me special medication to help me retain this pregnancy; and made plans to see me every two weeks.

After my series of miscarriages I was afraid to plan. Afraid to dream. But when I passed safely through my sixth month, I started preparing the baby's room: making blankets, toys, and trying to see *this baby* as a reality.

On November 13, 1969, after what seemed to be the world's longest pregnancy, Robert Grant made his appearance. There was a suspense-filled, eternity-long pause as we all waited for Robby to utter that first cry. Finally, triumphantly, the doctor held the baby up, and through tears of joy I saw my new son. He was bloody, wrinkled, and squalling. He was the most beautiful sight in the world.

The nurse took Robby out to meet his father, greeting him with, "Mr. Wheeler, here's your new son!" She looked at Dennis, who stands about five-foot-six, she looked at Robby, and finally she said, "And he's almost as big as you!" (Robby was really just under two feet long and ten pounds.)

Julie and Timmy had both been fair, Scandinavian-looking infants. Robby looked Mexican. There were gobs of black, curly hair on his head, his cheeks, his ears—all over.

This long-anticipated baby had a ten-pounder's appetite and an immature stomach. I was warned, "This condition often corrects itself, but there is the possibility of eventual surgery. Meanwhile, you can expect colic, projectile vomiting, and a very cranky baby."

The nurses seemed relieved to see our "little darling" leave their care, and Julie and Timmy were delighted to meet their new brother. Some of their delight disappeared, however, the tenth time they were told, "Please be quiet! The baby's sleeping."

On Thanksgiving Day, I took the twelve-day-old Robby in for the first of many trips to the emergency room. His navel was badly infected and had to be cauterized. Poor baby. He hurt so bad and cried so hard that he lost his breath and turned blue. Quickly, the doctor grabbed him up and cuddled the now-terrified infant until he started breathing again. For the next few years, whenever Robby was hurt that would happen. We knew he'd automatically start breathing again, but our babysitters had a tendency to panic.

Then there was the ever present colic. "Here's some medicine to help calm the spasms in his little stomach," we were told. "Rock him a lot. Love him a lot—oh, and ear plugs might help."

Robby's stomach would spasm. His little body would stiffen, and he'd howl with pain. He never seemed to stop crying. People often commented on his "ruddy" complexion; one day he stopped crying, and we discovered that he was really very fair.

We rocked, then rocked some more. I tried every possible way to hold and rock a baby: fast, slow, singing, over my knees, across my shoulder, walking. Mostly we just rocked. In desperation I put a warning sign over the doorbell: "If YOU wake the baby, you have to rock him!"

Dennis threatened to put an odometer on the rocker to keep track of the miles Robby and I put on that chair. Some days I felt that my rocking and holding him were all that kept Robby alive.

How much can one little body tolerate? I often asked myself and God. But we'd only begun to see just how much one chubby baby could tolerate. When Robby was two months old, I noticed something on his shoulder: a bump, slightly smaller than a halved golf ball, with red markings on the skin surface.

"Doctor, how could I have missed this and not seen it until now?" I asked.

"This is a subdural hemangeoma," the doctor explained. "The red mark is commonly called a strawberry mark, and no one notices these things before the second month. His seems to be growing rapidly. Better see the surgeon."

"It's a good thing you came to see me quickly," said the surgeon. "I'll set up a surgery date and we'll remove this thing. Before you leave today, I want the dermatologist to see this and confirm my opinion."

"Leave it alone! Should be gone by his fifth birthday," was the dermatologist's opinion. "These things are like icebergs, and we never know how deep we'll have to go or how bad a scar they'll leave until we get in there. Leave it alone."

The surgeon decided to postpone operating on Robby's

shoulder, but he gave me a stern warning: "If it ever gets hit or cut and starts bleeding, get him to emergency. Quick!"

On our next visit to the pediatrician, he was excited about Robby's weight gain. "As well as he's doing now, I think we can rule out the surgery on his stomach. He still has a lot of trouble with colic, but I think the immediate need for that surgery is over."

Dennis and I rejoiced—prematurely—"Maybe now things will calm down." *Then* Robby got his first ear infection, and I started to feel like a charter member of the "Trauma of the Month Club." After several bouts with the infections, we consulted another specialist. "If the infections continue with this severity," he said, "we'll have to put 'buttons' in his ears to help drain the fluid, and do a tonsillectomy."

The repeated infections left Robby with supersensitive hearing. When he wasn't crying with colic or an earache, he was screaming at high-pitched sounds: fire engines, howling dogs, doorbells, the vacuum cleaner, and one shrill-voiced neighbor.

Five-month-old Robby developed severe infections in both ears, and the liquid penicillin gave him such a serious case of diarrhea that he became dehydrated. The doctor told me, "We'll just take him off the liquid and give him a shot." Twenty-four hours later, Robby had an allergic reaction to the injection.

That same week Timmy was hospitalized with his head injury, and within a five day period I made seven doctor visits and fourteen phone calls (not even counting the hospitalization). As we waited to see if Tim would live, if he would have brain surgery, we were trying to get the right medicine for Robby's ear infections; treating the diarrhea and dehydration; and trying to get the allergic reaction under control.

Much to our surprise we all survived that week, and shortly after Timmy returned from the hospital, Dennis and I went away for a much needed weekend. Our good friends and neighbors, Mae and Robert Wilson, kept the three children.

We thoroughly and gratefully enjoyed our two day respite, but moments before we returned home, Robby scratched his eye with his little fingernail while playing in the playpen. The eye was badly inflamed when we arrived, so while Dennis unpacked, Robby and I made the very familiar trip to the doctor.

"He's scratched the cornea of his eye, but I think we caught it in time," the doctor said. "I'll medicate it and bandage it for twenty-four hours, and then we'll recheck. Treated this early, there's rarely any permanent damage."

By the time the doctor finished with Robby, I didn't know if I should laugh or cry. The white bandage over his eye covered half his face. Then they bandaged both hands so Robby wouldn't pull the essential bandage off his eye. The poor baby looked like a miniature disaster. I took him over to Wilson's to reassure them. But one look at the well-bandaged Robby and neither was very reassured.

About the time Robby's eye cleared up we noticed a new problem:

"Dennis, look at Robby's feet. What do they remind you of?"

"They seem to be turning in like Julie's," he answered.

Oh, dear God! Not that, too. Please, not that.

"Mrs. Wheeler, Robby does seem to toe in. We'll try this night brace, and in a year he should be fine." The orthopedist echoed the words we'd heard about Julie almost eight years before.

Dear God, that's just what they said about Julie, and she's still in braces, still no better. Him too?

Robby started walking on his first birthday and fell constantly. He was a mass of bumps, bruises, and broken teeth.

"Robby's teeth are like chalk," the dentist explained. "They have no enamel, and we'll have to watch them carefully as he's still too young to treat."

What next, Lord?

"Next" turned out to be a very unexpected pregnancy. I couldn't use the Pill, so we'd decided to use an IUD (intrauterine device; supposedly 90 percent safe). When I got the very familiar symptoms I called the doctor.

The doctor humored me, quoted statistics, and ran the test.

"Negative!"

The symptoms persisted, and so did I. They ran another test.

"Congratulations!"

Julie was in her leg braces and making little improvement, Timmy was slowly recovering from his injury, and we knew that in a few months Robby would be wearing braces like Julie's.

"Why now?"

"I know this pregnancy was unplanned," the doctor said, "and we can remove the IUD now and that will probably terminate this pregnancy."

Suddenly, Dennis and I became very protective of this unplanned baby. After all the miscarriages, and in spite of the awkward timing, neither of us could consider terminating a pregnancy.

I went in for my three months checkup and was told, "Everything is fine!" That night I started hemorrhaging, and for the next month we lived on an emotional seesaw.

I'd go to bed for a few days. The bleeding would stop. The doctor would tell me, "I think you're going to make it. You can get up now."

I'd hemorrhage again.

Julie took care of Robby. Timmy sort of took care of himself. Dennis did the housework and took care of me. I stayed in bed and prayed.

Dennis was remarkable throughout that horrible month.

He was working eight hours and had a long commute, yet he still came home and scrubbed floors, cleaned the oven, washed diapers, and encouraged me.

Things calmed down for a while, and the doctor still thought there was a chance for this baby. We were finally feeling hopeful and encouraged.

The hemorrhaging started again, this time with such intensity that I was alarmed. I went around and kissed the sleeping children—one last time?—and then we left for the hospital. After four hours of hard labor, my seventh pregnancy ended.

Even after four miscarriages, I never got the knack of thinking of my loss as "a thing," "a fetus," "not really a baby." Those were all the terms the well-intentioned doctors used.They always refused to tell us the sex of the fetus, assuming that it was easier to think of "it" rather than a boy or girl. But their theory just didn't work. From the very first I knew that I had a living being growing inside me, not some "it"; a tiny embryonic person, not a thing.

In my head I knew that losing a full-term baby would be more painful. But *in my heart* this loss hurt. Well-meaning friends and relatives added to the pain with: "It's best, they're usually defective"; "You don't need any more"; "It wasn't planned anyway"; "Aren't you lucky you weren't further along?" The friends that helped most just simply and quietly said, "I know you're hurting, and I'm sorry."

When I went in for my next checkup the doctor warned, "I really recommend against any further pregnancies. You and your husband need to take permanent measures against this ever happening again."

Dennis and I had many long talks and reviewed all our options. "Bonnie, maybe when things calm down around here we can consider adopting a fourth child. Meanwhile, I'm going to have a vasectomy. I don't want you going through this again."

I was grateful to Dennis for his thoughtfulness and understanding, but I was angry with God. I had prayed so hard for Him to save the baby that when I did miscarry I couldn't see it as part of His perfect plan. I had asked and He had either just answered no or didn't care.

The news about Julie's cerebral palsy, the pain of Timmy's injury, the endless traumas with Robby—none of them hurt with the same intensity I felt when it seemed that God had turned His back on me, no longer listened and no longer cared.

I was run down, emotionally and physically exhausted; my blood count was low from the weeks of hemorrhaging, and I wasn't thinking clearly. Just reacting. Drained. Empty. For months I thought I was still mourning the loss of my baby. I was really grieving for my imagined loss of God.

Robby turned two, and to "celebrate" the orthopedist put him into full-length cable braces just like Julie's. The doctor continually assured me that Robby didn't have cerebral palsy, but seeing the exact same patterns repeated, the fear remained.

We no sooner got his legs taken care of than it was time to revisit the dentist. "Now that Robby is two, we have to do something about these teeth," the dentist said. "We're going to cap them before they get worse. It'll be considered oral surgery and require hospitalization."

Our next-door neighbor, Jeanette Widegren, drove us to the hospital, helped me find the labs, and stayed until Robby was settled in his room. Then she went home to take care of Julie and Timmy.

Once Robby was settled down and the nurses left us alone, Robby found a chair by the window, turned his back to me, and refused to speak.

"What's wrong, Robby?"

"I not talk to you."

Dennis, Julie, and Bonnie, a
family of three in 1963.

Timmy in 1966, getting
started early.

"Grammy" Wheeler, Timmy, and
Julie at Easter 1969.

Robby the sailor in 1970.

Becky playing at Glankler School.

Yasiuki, Robby, Becky, Julie, and Junko—the Wheelers and their friends from Japan.

The brothers Wheeler, Benji, Robby, and Timmy. Photo by Gary Jones.

Melissa and Norma Johnson at Melissa's 10th birthday party.

"Look, Mom, we're twins!"
Photo by Dave Sevilla.

Above: A family portrait in 1976, before Melissa joined the family;
Dennis holding the smiling Becky, Julie, Robby, Bonnie holding Benji,
and Timmy. Photo by Llyod Ostergaard.

Below: "Christmas Story 1978" at the Wheeler's. Dennis and Benji,
Bonnie and Melissa, Becky, Robby, Julie, and Timmy. Images by Tovic.

"Aw, please. What's wrong?"

Long pause. No answer.

"I wait for Daddy come get me. *He* not leave me here."
(How come poor Mommy always gets the blame?)

Dennis came after work and stayed with Robby until Robby fell asleep. I was back early the next morning. The nurse had just given Robby a shot, and he was crying. "Now don't let him walk around," she said. "This will make him drowsy, and he might fall and get hurt."

Robby was soon sedated and groggy. The orderly came to take him up to the operating room, and Robby went into hysterics. "Mother, why don't you come along with us to the elevator?" said the huge orderly; he was a real softy for crying children. I held Robby's hand, and the orderly wheeled the gurney toward the elevator. This tiny, heavily sedated child saw that elevator, saw that I wasn't going in it with him, and started fighting frantically to get off that gurney and into my arms.

The picture we made was almost comical: this tiny, semiconscious child, a huge black orderly, and me. The orderly and I tried to stuff this little kid onto the gurney and into the elevator, and the little kid was winning!

An elderly lady chose this inopportune time to amble by. She stopped, watched our struggle, glared at us, gave an audible "tsk! tsk!" and scurried away. Probably to report us.

Robby had so many allergy problems that I was very concerned about his reaction to the anesthetic, but there were no real problems. Robby did spend the afternoon vomiting from the anesthetic, and his gums were raw and bloody. He kept yelling, "I want me Daddy!"

After Robby's hospital stay, we prepared for and enjoyed Christmas. Shortly after the new year some unknown "plague" struck:

"Mrs. Wheeler, you have a measles virus."

"Mrs. Wheeler, this ear infection, sinus infection, and the arthritic pains are all a side effect of the virus."

"Mrs. Wheeler, Julie, Tim, and Robby all have a viral rash."

"Veterinarian's office? This is Mrs. Wheeler. I have three kids with a measles-type virus, and now the lizard and parakeet are sick. Can they catch the measles? Hello?"

The pets died. The three kids and I survived. If you take a bucket of water and pour it over a rock, there's no real effect. But a small, constant drip of water can wear away the biggest rock. And I was wearing away fast.

I had been able to handle the big "splash" made by Julie's cerebral palsy and Timmy's injury, but the constant "drip" during Robby's first two years was almost more than I could handle.

During that short period, Robby had twenty-three ear infections, severe colic, an immature stomach, projectile vomiting, an infected cord, the growth on his shoulder, oral surgery, a scratched cornea, the virus, and leg braces. And just for good measure, he was allergic to chocolate, penicillin, and milk.

I felt like a drowning victim who knows she's going under for the last time. Once again, I yelled out my frustrations and fears to God.

Hey God! Do You hear me? I've had it! You promised, No more than I can handle. This is it! One more problem will be the end of me. I can't take any more. You know that "straw that broke the camel's back"? That's me—now. *No more straws! No more problems.* Please God!...*Please.*"

5
Interim

WHEN DENNIS AND I felt the need for some relief from the pressures at home, we volunteered to work at the local drug abuse center. Although we were really just trading one set of pressures for another, it was a change and kept us from drowning in the morass of our home pressures. We attended special first-aid classes; learned drug identification; handled "hot line" calls; detoxed overdoses; and participated in encounter groups. We worked out our schedules so that one of us was always home with the children—always the main priority. Dennis was at the center on Saturday nights, and I was there on Mondays.

The crisis center time was one of great learning for both of us. Our "straight" friends gave us a rough time about working for "your dopers." They thought that our working with those troubled teens implied our approval of their actions. Dennis and I were learning an important lesson for our future: doing what *we knew* was right might not always win us the approval of others.

Dennis had always been the quiet type, and our one conflict was my begging, "Talk to me." In the encounter groups, we learned many important lessons in communication. We learned to talk to others and, most important, how to talk with each other about the things that really matter.

During those years we opened our home on several occasions to troubled kids who needed a temporary home. We all enjoyed these stays (from three days to three weeks) so much that a trend started that we came to love. There have been touring musical groups; kids recovering from overdoses; victims of broken homes; Army nurses; missionaries; and foreign exchange students.

Our first experience was with Up With People. They're a touring musical group whose members spend the night in the local homes (more interesting in Mexico or Hawaii than in Fremont, I'm sure). We had two black girls and a blonde. The blonde was from an Iowa farm, and the other two were from Alaska and Bermuda. The Alaskan saw her first Eskimo and ate Baked Alaska for the first time after she joined the tour.

When the girls left, we were curious about Timmy's and Julie's reactions and especially wanted to know any racial comments or concerns.

"What did you think of the girls?" we asked.

"They were great!" was their spontaneous reply.

"Well, Mommy," Julie added, "I really felt sorry for that one girl, and I sure hope I never look like her."

Uh-oh!

"Daddy, that blonde girl had pimples all over her face and they were awful! I sure hope I have skin like *the other two* when I'm a teenager."

During their stay, one of the girls wanted to go to church on Sunday. There was a new one near our home, and I offered to take our guest. Fremont Neighborhood Church (Christian and Missionary Alliance) was warm and friendly, and I hoped to return.

Shortly after my first visit, Bob and Mae Wilson started attending and invited Julie to go along to Sunday school with their daughter Jenny. Occasionally, we would attend a special service or program that Julie was in. Dennis was still working Saturday nights at the crisis center and was getting home at 3

A.M.; we told Pastor Wes Jeske when he visited, "Regular church attendance is out for us now."

Shortly after Robby's second birthday we received a call: "Hi! I'm Darlene Schmierer from Fremont Neighborhood Church. Sunday night is our 'Hospitality Sunday,' and we'd like you and your family to join us after the evening service."

We weren't sure what to expect, but we accepted the invitation. After church, we gathered up the kids and followed Mel and Darlene home. Much to our surprise we had a delightful evening. The Schmierers lived a few blocks from us, had three children near the same ages as ours, and their kids attended the same school as ours.

When I told Darlene of Robby's coming hospitalization, she promised to pray and offered her help. I was touched—and impressed—the next month when she remembered and called. "I just want you to know we're praying for Robby," she said, "and if there's anything I can do to help, please let me know."

Although I had attended church all my life, it hadn't always been a positive experience, and it certainly never united our family in the way I saw at the Schmierer home.

"Your church is too emotional!" my grandfather would scream (never realizing the irony of *his* emotional state).

"Well, your church is too liberal!" my grandmother would counterattack.

A typical Sunday afternoon conversation from my childhood was anything but peaceful or unifying. I would go to Sunday school with Pop, church with Mom. Then I'd spend the rest of the day listening to their arguing. When I entered junior high I declared my spiritual independence and ended their tug-of-war. I found an evangelical church and walked—in peace—by myself.

I wanted nothing to do with their weekly debates, and my diary records, "It seems to me that church and God and religion should bring a family together. Not tear it apart. I'll never let that happen in my home.''

I wrote it down. Remembered it. Believed it. And for the past few years we'd lived it. While Timmy was an infant, we'd attended church regularly. Unfortunately, we joined a church more interested in checks than souls. Dennis knew their attitude was wrong. We quit the church and he blamed God: ''If that's what churches are like, who needs them?''

I was determined that church wouldn't tear our family apart. If Dennis wouldn't go, then neither would I. At home I read my Bible and prayed. We occasionally had family devotions. But we didn't go to church. I didn't grow. Dennis still didn't know the Lord.

That fall of 1972, I reached the point where I just couldn't cope any longer. Timmy's hyperactivity was at its worst, and the strain of trying to cope with the children's various physical problems and meet their special emotional needs was wearing me down. My nerves were shot from the constant strains of the past few years, and I was physically and emotionally drained. When I explained my family situation to the doctor, he prescribed tranquilizers without any hesitation. Even they didn't help.

Since the last miscarriage I had felt that my prayers weren't being answered. I still had an emptiness that neither Dennis, the children, nor the crisis center could fill.

I had accepted Jesus Christ as my personal Savior when I was very young, and throughout a very painful childhood and adolescence He was the ''glue'' that held me together. Now that I felt that glue no longer there, I was coming apart at the seams.

When Dennis and I were married, I knew he didn't have a personal relationship with Jesus. But he was ''such a good person'' that I felt confident *I* could easily lead him to the

Lord. Then as we went from one trauma to another, I discovered that *I* not only couldn't save Dennis, but I also could just barely keep myself afloat.

During my personal bout with depression and discouragement, God used two simple things to turn me around and back to Him: a bumper sticker and a record.

The bumper sticker? "If God seems far away, who moved?" I started asking myself that question and many others:

"Is this emptiness my fault?"

"Has God turned His back on me, or have I turned away from Him?"

"Is God still there?"

"Is He still waiting? Loving me?"

Then my grandmother sent me a record:

"Is your burden heavy as you bear it all alone?"

(*It's too heavy, Lord.*)

"Does the road you travel harbor danger yet unknown?"

(*Will Julie's legs improve? Will Timmy ever calm down? Will Robby's legs ever be strong, sturdy, and straight?*)

"Are you growing weary in the struggle of it all?"

(*Oh, yes, Lord! so very, very weary.*)

The musical questions all applied to me. I had answered them all, but what was *the* answer? As the chorus began, I sat on the edge of my chair and prayerfully, searchingly listened, oblivious to the tears streaming down my face.

"He is always there, hearing every prayer, faithful and
true.

...When you get discouraged just remember what to do—
Reach out to Jesus, He's reaching out to you."

(*Oh, God! Are You really there? Waiting? Reaching? Loving?*)

REACH OUT TO JESUS by Ralph Carmichael
Copyright 1968 by LEXICON MUSIC, INC. ASCAP
All rights reserved. International copyright secured.
Used by permission.

In that fall of 1972, I knew that I couldn't cope anymore—by myself. I finally realized that I'd reached *my limit*. I went to Dennis and said, "I love you so very much, and I don't want to pressure you. But I have to get things right with God. Maybe through this church I can. I don't know if this is the answer, but I do know I can't go on like this. I have to try."

After I talked with Dennis I talked to God. *Lord, I don't know if this is the church for me. I don't know if this is the answer, if this is the way back to You. But Lord, I know that there's something missing and I can't find it on my own. I finally realize that I can't save myself, much less Dennis. I turn him over to You, Lord. You'll have to take care of him. I'm just too tired.*

For the next few Sunday mornings, the kids and I left Dennis sleeping (he was still working at the crisis center) and went to church. During Thanksgiving and Christmas, there were special services and programs planned for almost every Sunday evening service.

Dennis would read my bulletin. Julie would say, "Oh, Daddy, we're having a Sunday school program and I'm in it"; or, "I wish you could hear the choir sing."

By Christmas we had attended five weeks of evening services *together as a family*. I was so afraid that, once the holidays were over and there were no more children's programs or special music, Dennis would start staying home again. To my surprise and delight, Dennis said, "Let's start 1973 off right. I see there's a communion service tonight."

It was a "regular" service. There was no special music; Pastor Jeske said nothing new or unique; there was no fancy program or entertainment. But our lives would never be the same again.

We entered the church,
walked down the aisle to the third row on the right.

We sat down in very ordinary—and uncomfortable—metal chairs.

Pastor spoke.

The bread was passed. We ate. We prayed.

The cup was passed. We drank. We prayed.

We prayed again.

We went home.

"Dennis! Dennis, I have to talk to you."

"Bonnie! Bonnie, I have to talk to you."

"Dennis, tonight I—"

"Bonnie, tonight I—"

When we let each other speak, when we finally listened:

"Bonnie, tonight I asked Jesus to forgive my sins and come into my heart and be my personal Savior!"

"Oh, Dennis! That's so wonderful! Dennis, tonight I rededicated my life to the Lord and started a fresh walk with Him."

Neither of us remembers what was said that night.

Yet neither of us can forget what happened.

The peace that came.

The changes that were wrought.

The blessings that would pour forth as we each listened to the still, small voice of the Holy Spirit.

Early Monday morning I called Darlene Schmierer to tell her our good news. "Praise the Lord!" she said. "We've been praying for this to happen since that first evening we met you."

Mel started a one-on-one discipleship program with Dennis that continued for the next two years, and I joined a Bible study-prayer group with Darlene.

As we grew closer to the Lord, we felt more estranged from the crisis center and more frustrated with the restrictions that prevented us from talking about Jesus. At one time we had thought of the crisis center as an "arrival," as a goal. We were discovering that it was only *the training* God used to prepare us for what He had planned, not *the destination*.

As one phase of our lives closed, another opened up.

I had been a Christian so many more years than Dennis (albeit not a growing one) that I was afraid of usurping Dennis's rightful position as spiritual leader of our home. The Lord blessed that concern and gave Dennis such a hunger for the Word that Dennis immediately assumed his place as our spiritual leader. God had been patiently waiting for me to turn over all the controls to Him.

As we put our spiritual house in order, we had to do some work on our finances, too. "Bonnie, finances are just too tight," Dennis said one night. "I've asked Bob Wilson for a part-time job at the pizza parlor."

Dennis's job started the same week as Pastor Jeske's membership classes, and I was constantly amazed at Dennis's new commitment. He would get in at 3 A.M. on Sunday, sleep a few hours, and be at church by 9:30 A.M. He was still getting up early on Friday mornings to meet Mel for their discipleship time, and every night (no matter how late) Dennis would study his Bible.

During those early months there were numerous times when I'd grow concerned about Dennis's schedule and lack of sleep. I would stop where I was and pray, "Lord, be with Dennis right now. Strengthen him and let him feel Your presence."

The next morning Dennis would tell me, "Right at midnight [or whatever time I'd been praying], I was so tired I couldn't see straight. I felt a rush of strength and energy come through me, and I'd have no more trouble."

During that first year we heard Ord Morrow of "Back to the Bible"; Howard Jones of the Billy Graham organization held a series of meetings at our church; and we attended the Institute in Basic Youth Conflicts.

We grew. We learned. We absorbed. We listened to Pastor Jeske's sermons on *loving others, claiming God's promises,* and *stepping out in faith,* little realizing how we would soon be putting those sermons into action.

As this new dimension was added to our life, our marriage blossomed and matured in a fresh and beautiful way. Of all the sorrows and joys we had shared—the births of the three children, their physical problems, the miscarriages—nothing gave us the closeness and blessing of being able to share our mutual love for Jesus. It was a wonderful time of learning, growing, and healing.

The Lord took me in His arms and welcomed me home; He loved me; gave me a time of rest; healed my shattered nerves; and daily I read His promises:

I have ransomed you; I have called
you by name; you are mine. When you
go through deep waters and great trouble,
I will be with you.

Isaiah 43:1-2

Nowhere in those promises did He tell His people that there would be no more trouble. He did promise to always go through those troubles with them. Always together. I won't ever be alone. I won't ever have to cope in my own strength.

For I can do everything God asks
me to with the help of Christ who
gives me the strength and power.

Philippians 4:13

For God has said, "I will never, *never*
fail you nor forsake you."

Hebrews 13:5

We were beginning to see Acts 16:31 in action ("Believe

on the Lord Jesus and you will be saved, and your entire household."), as one by one the children accepted Jesus as their own personal Savior: Julie had accepted Jesus during Vacation Bible School, and even though she was still wearing her braces she was able to say, "God has a very special purpose for making me this way. I don't know what it is, but someday I will."

God had even handpicked the perfect Sunday school teacher for Julie. Sharon Sartori had polio, wears heavy leg braces, and teaches from a wheelchair. She cheerfully accepts her physical challenges, drives a car, works as a secretary, counsels at camp, and loves the Lord.

As Julie's love and knowledge of Jesus grew, along with Sharon's loving example, so grew Julie's self-assurance and acceptance.

We had a series of children's meetings that fall, and after one of them Timmy came running out to the car. "Mommy! Daddy!" he shouted. "I asked Jesus into my heart!"

Timmy was on medication and was responding, like a thirsty sponge, to the love and acceptance he was receiving at church. "I got a candy bar for being the quietest," he said one Sunday. "Somebody really said I was good!"

Robby was out of his leg braces by his fourth birthday; his legs were strong, sturdy, and straight. Most of his medical problems were improving, and he was a charmer.

As 1973 came to a close I wrote, "This is the first time I can remember the old year being so beautiful that I'm almost afraid for the new year to start. Dennis and I have grown in the Lord. The kids' health problems are so much better, and I have this very strong feeling of anticipation that God has something very special and specific planned for us."

Shortly after the new year began, God started giving me clues on "that something special and specific":

Enlarge your house; build on additions;
spread out your home! For you will soon be
bursting at the seams!
                              Isaiah 54:2

And if, as my representatives, you give
even a cup of cold water to a little child,
you will surely be rewarded.
                              Matthew 10:42

I want you to share your food with the hungry
and bring right into your own home those who
are helpless, poor and destitute.
                              Isaiah 58:7

We had talked years ago about adopting a child, but I was
always either pregnant, recovering, or caring for sick children.
Dennis and I had many long talks and prayer sessions about
this renewed possibility. I started calling adoption agencies to
gather information. We had always assumed that we would
adopt an infant, but my very first phone call destroyed that
myth.

After that first conversation with the adoption worker,
Dennis and I got down to some very serious prayer, discussion, and reevaluation. The more we prayed, the more certain
we became that the Lord wanted us to adopt a physically handicapped child. He was showing us that the experiences we
had with Julie, Timmy, and Robby were His perfect preparation for the ministry He was planning for us.

Once we made the decision to adopt a handicapped child,
Dennis and I had peace that we were within God's will. The
reactions from everyone else, however, were very negative.

Social workers: "Do you really think you can handle it?"

Friends: "You'll finally have some free time when Robby
starts school. You're nuts!"

Family: "Take care of the three you've got! You can't afford them, much less another."

After listening to all of that, we talked to Mel and Darlene Schmierer. Their middle child, Gina, is adopted. She has an American Indian heritage, is adorable, and calls me "Aunt Bonnie." The Schmierers had also had a bad experience with troubled foster children and could give us a realistic view of both good and bad.

In spite of the many negative reactions, we both felt stronger each day that this was God's will. We were so convinced that this was the right thing that we were afraid *not* to proceed.

> Knowing what is right to do
> and then not doing it is sin.
>
> James 4:17

On February 19, 1974, we attended our first adoption meeting. It wasn't encouraging, but we talked, prayed, and held family conferences about what we wanted and thought we could *realistically* handle. We then requested:

a girl: "to balance out the family"
under four: "younger than Robby"
physically handicapped: "We'd prefer cerebral palsy"
race: "Who cares?" (Timmy did request "a black girl with a blond Afro, so I won't be the only blond in the family.")

Then we prayed, "Lord, somewhere there is a little girl that You've already selected for us. A little girl that needs us. That we can welcome, love, and teach about You. Start now preparing her heart for us, and ours for her. And Lord, please bring her to us in such a way that we'll have *no doubts* that she's *the one* You selected just for us. Amen."

When Dennis and I first felt the Lord's leading, we knew nothing about the finances of adoption. We knew there was an adoption fee charged by the agency. There would be a lawyer's fee and the actual expense of caring for a special child.

By this time Dennis had quit his second job, and money was tight. We just kept on trusting. Practically and logically we'd start discussing all of this. One of us would ask, "But how can *we* possibly afford one more expense?"

The other would reply, *"We* can't possibly afford it, but *God can."*

In March we received a phone call from the adoption agency. "Hi!" a friendly voice said. "Your adoption application has been processed, and I'm the worker assigned to your case. Reading your application, I see that you've had a lot of physical problems with your children. Are you certain you want another?"

The next week we met her for the first of many interviews; hearts pounding, we sat across from her desk and waited.

Skeptically, she again asked, "How can you possibly want to take on another child? Especially a handicapped child, after all you've been through?"

Dennis—the master of understatement—looked her in the eyes and honestly answered, "Gee, it hasn't been *that* bad." Shaking her head, the mystified social worker turned to me and waited for my answer.

"I feel like a survivor of the Titanic!" I said. "I think we've been through a lot! But the secret is, 'We've been through.' We've experienced. It would be a bigger problem to place a child with special needs in a family that had never experienced anything worse than diaper rash. We've been there. We're coming through it. And now we have a chance to take all that experience and pain and use it in a positive way."

The interviews continued: separately, together, and with the children. There wasn't an area of our lives we weren't questioned about. It was nerve-wracking, prying, at times embarrassing—but very, very necessary.

As the home study progressed, never fast enough for me,

we heard from social workers from Chicago to Los Angeles. We never prayed for God to specifically give us a child; just, "Please take care of this child and find her the best possible home."

Time after time, it wasn't us. We were beginning to feel that our ministry was going to be praying homeless children into adoptive homes.

In June, our worker briefly mentioned a little girl that she had hoped would work out for us. "She is three, black, and has cerebral palsy," she said. "Her mother has a drug problem and can't take care of her. The judge hasn't released the child for adoption yet."

That summer I prayed daily for our unseen daughter *and* this other child. As the adoption process slowly moved on, we were asked to work as camp deans at our denomination's summer camp. C.B. Stack, our youth pastor, asked if we would go with him the week he would be director. Instead of disciplining three kids, we'd have 150. Julie was in a cabin with her friends, and the two boys stayed with us.

The camp setting, in the midst of California's redwoods, is breathtaking. It was a welcome break from the constant thoughts, plans, and interviews concerning the adoption.

Each evening Robby would wait for the evening message to start, and then he would curl up in my lap and go to sleep. One evening, C.B. asked the campers who wanted to accept Jesus or rededicate their lives to raise their hands. Many children stayed after.

I took Timmy and Robby to our cabin to tuck them in and hear their prayers, while Dennis started his evening chores. I kissed Timmy, and as I zipped up his sleeping bag he said, "Mommy I raised my hand tonight and rededicated my life to Jesus."

With tears in my eyes, I tucked Timmy in and prayed with him. Afterward, I crossed the room to Robby's bed. "Mommy,

I stayed awake tonight and raised my hand,'' he said.

''What for, Robby?''

''C.B. said if you want to ask Jesus into your heart to raise your hand. I did, and I do.'' Robby and I prayed together, and C.B. came in and talked to him.

C.B. told me, ''He may be young, but he sure knew what he was doing tonight.''

God added two friends to our lives that summer: ''Little Doc'' and ''Marsha the Missionary.'' I had an unforgettable and precious walk with Doc. She's under five feet tall, is a cross between a teddy bear and Corrie Ten Boom, and is nearing eighty.

Doc and I were walking through the redwoods, and she took my hand and said, ''This is just like it will be when we get to heaven. I will be there first, and I'll be the first to welcome you home. I'll hold your hand just like this and show you all over heaven.''

The day after we returned from camp we got a phone call from our social worker. ''Remember that little girl I told you about earlier?'' (Remember? For two months I'd been praying for her daily.) ''We have to find a new foster home for her, but we still don't know when the judge will free her for adoption. Do you think you would want to take a risk? We can place her as a 'preadopt' and hope you'll eventually be able to adopt her. Talk it over with Dennis and call me back.''

Before she hung up, the worker gave me the rest of the information: ''The little girl was three in June. She has cerebral palsy [spastic quadriparaplegic]. She's black and Oriental, has very poor sitting balance, emotional problems, and she'll never walk. Oh—the doctors think she might be retarded.''

Dennis and I talked together and prayed. For months we'd been burdened for this child and praying for both her *and* our unseen daughter.

"Yes! We'll see her."

An appointment was made for us to see the child that weekend. In Friday's mail there was a picture for us. As prepared as I thought I was, when I saw the severity of her handicap I almost called and canceled.

Lord?

6
Becky

"HI! ARE YOU GOING to be my new mommy and daddy?"

When we were greeted so cheerfully by Becky, I had to stop and ask myself, *Is this the child we were told about? Retarded with many emotional problems? What a difference between the official record and the actual reality of this child!*

She was so much prettier than the picture that I'd seen and been so scared by. Becky had a soft Afro, lovely carmel colored skin, and a big smile. I could see glimpses of her Oriental heritage in the lighter skin and the soft—not quite kinky—Afro.

She crawled over to me and started bombarding me with questions:

"Why don't you pick me up?"

"Do you like little girls?"

"Where do you live?"

"Do you have any kids?"

While she was asking her nonstop questions, I was trying vainly to answer them and scrutinize her at the same time.

With that speech and curiosity, there's no way she's retarded. She's really tight and spastic. She's very pretty. Every time she laughs she falls over. Is she the one, Lord?

I had no idea how nerve-wracking being interrogated and approved—I hoped —by a small child could be. Finally, with an imperious "Put me down!" Becky crawled over to Dennis and started giving him the "third degree":

"Hi! Are you going to be my new daddy?"

"Pick me up!"

"What's this in your pocket?"

"Do you live with *her?*"

"Can I keep this card?"

"Is this your name on here?"

"When will you come back to see me?"

"Will you bring your kids?"

It was rather like being interviewed by a rapid-fire machine gun. Becky was obviously bright, very alert, supercurious, and enchanted with Dennis (a sure sign of good taste). Once she had asked Dennis, "Will you be my new daddy?" he was hooked and had no doubts that she was *the one.*

Becky had taken a business card from Dennis's shirt pocket and asked to keep it. The next morning I called the foster mother and asked, "What was Becky's reaction? What did she think of us?"

"Becky kept that business card in her hand all night. If she clinches her fist her toes curl up. This morning I couldn't get her shoes on, checked her hands, and there was the card. 'What's this?' I asked."

"This is my new daddy's name!"

Our social worker called that afternoon. "Hi! How did the visit go?" she asked. "Becky's foster mother has had lots of experience with preplacement visits, and I'll leave most of the visiting arrangements to you two. There should be several visits back and forth; she'll stay alone with you several different times and spend the night several times. From what I've heard of her, it will probably take a lot of visits and a lot of time. Be patient."

In further conversations with Becky's foster mother, we learned more about Becky's background: "Her mother was very young, and she had a drug problem. We're Becky's fifth placement. [She'd just turned three!] Becky goes into

Children's Hospital every week for therapy; her sitting balance is very poor; she'll have extensive surgery on her legs and feet when she's five; and she's already had four eye surgeries.

"Becky can't tolerate change at all," the foster mother continued. "She had her last eye surgery in March and was so traumatized by the whole thing that she's been on medication ever since. When Becky gets nervous or upset, she literally gets 'uptight'—so tight we can't even get her dressed. We'd better plan on at least two months of visits to make the transition as smooth as possible."

After we had seen Becky and gotten more information on her, we talked with the children to give them our first impressions of Becky; and we made plans for a brief family visit that weekend. The kids were all bubbling over with excitement and anticipation at finally getting to see this child we had all talked, thought, and prayed about for so many months.

"Hi!" Becky cheerfully greeted the kids. I picked her up, gave her a hug, and carried her to the car. Our plans included a stop for ice cream cones and a short trip to the park. As we drove away from the foster home, Becky grew quieter and her thumb stayed in her mouth. We picked up the ice cream cones and found a nearby park. The kids all sat on the grass, eating their ice cream and watching Becky. She tried to suck her thumb and eat her ice cream but only succeeded in falling over every few seconds and getting herself covered with chocolate. She was a mess and I was a nervous wreck.

A few days later Becky's foster mother brought her to our house for a brief visit. During the next visit the foster mother had a cup of coffee and then said, "Becky, you stay here for a while. I'm going shopping and I'll be back in a few hours. OK?"

Becky immediately jammed her thumb into her mouth again. (Her thumb isn't an ordinary one—it's more like a computer hookup; she plugs it in and starts thinking.)

"OK!" she finally answered. Then she scampered off to play with the kids. Becky liked playing with the boys and was very obviously fascinated by Julie.

"Julie wears braces bigger than mine. And she walks!"

"Let me see your dolly!"

"Can I watch you ride your bike?"

"Read me this book!"

That first "left alone" visit was such a success that we planned an overnighter for the weekend. Becky's foster mother gave me more information on the "emotional problems" that the social worker had only briefly mentioned.

"Becky doesn't like to be left alone, and she cries whenever she is. She even follows me to the bathroom and screams when I close the door. If she hears a door slam, she startles and screams. Some days she wakes up and it's just a bad day—cause unknown—and she'll cry *all day*. The reason the doctors labeled her retarded? When she goes in to be examined, she screams throughout the whole exam and they can't test her.

"Becky's just started therapy because the neurologist felt she couldn't handle being around any new people; most children with cerebral palsy start therapy much younger."

By the time I got all the necessary information on Becky, I was frantically rereading those promises the Lord had given us. I was scared, but we both still felt confident that this was *the child* the Lord wanted us to have. We had reached the point of needing another family conference:

"Well, kids, what do you think of Becky?" Dennis asked. "Would you like her for your sister?"

"I think she's cute!"

"Let's get her!"

"When can she move in?"

"Kids," I interjected when I got the chance, "some people can be very prejudiced, especially against black people.''

"What's *prejudice* mean?" asked Robby.

"It must mean dumb!" Timmy answered.

"What would you boys do if someone called your sister a nigger?" we asked.

We waited for our Christian kids to answer. The two boys shouted in unison, "We'd knock their blocks off!"

After the family talk I went to Julie and said, "Honey, before Becky comes to stay, we want to talk to you. There will be some problems with Becky's adjusting, and she really likes you. The first time you get angry you're probably going to feel guilty. Don't! Whenever you have negative feelings, come and talk to us. We won't think you're horrid, and it'll be a lot better for you than keeping it all inside."

We held many family conferences and individual talks with the children, and then it was time for the big test—Becky's first overnight visit.

"Hi, Becky! Are you ready to spend the night at our house?" I asked.

"I'm not spending the night with *you*," she answered. "I'm spending the night with Julie."

We went shopping that evening to pick out the paint for Becky's room, and after our shopping trip Becky got to sleep with Julie. I only fixed her favorite foods, she was never left alone, and it was a terrific visit.

Early the morning after Becky had left, I called Becky's foster mother. "Well, how did she like it?" I said. "Was she upset? Does she want to come back? What did she say?" (I was starting to sound like Becky.)

"Bonnie, I'm afraid we have a problem," the foster mother told me.

"Oh, no! What?"

"You know how we'd planned on six weeks to two months for a transition period? Well, I don't think Becky can handle that. She came home and asked me for a paper bag. *'I'm gonna pack my things and move to my new home!'* she told me.''

Later that day our worker called to say, ''I've been talking to Becky's foster mother, and we're afraid for Becky to stay at such an emotional peak much longer. Are you ready for her now?''

When the adults in Becky's world got together and compared notes, we discovered that part of her insecurity over the past few months had been caused by the foster care situation she was in. Her foster family took in infants and only kept them for the few months before their adoptions. Becky was their first exception. Becky never saw the new homes of the babies when they were adopted. One day the latest would be gone and Becky would ask, ''Where did he go?''

The only answer she was ever given was a brief, ''He was adopted.''

She'd pop that computer thumb in her mouth and try to sort this puzzle out. *What's adoption? Where do the babies disappear to? Where do they go?* No one realized how bright she was or thought to explain the process to her. ''She's too young to understand; she's only three'' was the rationale.

After her first visit with us, Becky turned to her foster mother, heaved a big sigh of relief, and said, ''So that's adoption!''

As we received more information on the legal and financial aspects of adoption, we were also sighing in relief. We were still walking by faith about the finances involved and just kept telling each other, ''God will provide a way.''

God's way seemed to be declaring an open season on miracles:

''When you adopt a child with known physical problems you get full medical coverage, and whatever Medi-Cal doesn't cover, Crippled Children's Services will. That will cover braces, surgery, doctors, wheelchairs, and therapy,'' the social worker explained. "We waive the adoption fee for special adoptions, and since Becky's coming in as a preadoptive foster child, we'll pay you the regular foster care board rate until the adoption is finalized.''

The foster mother called and told us, "By the way, Becky will be bringing all of her clothes and toys, so you won't need to buy any of those.''

Next was a phone call from a couple at church: "We hear you need an extra bed, and we have one. When can you pick it up?''

We took a giant step of faith, and God blessed that step of faith abundantly.

On September 6, 1974, Rebecca Anne Wheeler *came home.* Her toys were waiting in her newly painted room, and she brought paper bags filled with her clothes. Becky's foster mother gave us a scrapbook she'd made for Becky; it would be an important link to Becky's past.

The foster mother and two social workers brought Becky to our house (that way we didn't go and *take* her away); we signed a ream of papers and became the parents of four children.

Becky moved in a month sooner than our man-made schedules called for. Everyone else was surprised —astonished—at Becky's enthusiasm and excitement. Just two months before she had been hysterical at changing campsites. Now here she was changing families, cities, and homes with delight.

We were the only ones not surprised. We saw it as a direct answer to my daily prayers over the past nine months. *Lord,* I had prayed, *somewhere You have a very special little girl all picked out for us. Prepare her heart and ours.*

And He did.

Robby started kindergarten the Monday after Becky arrived, and Becky and I started our weekly trips to Children's

Hospital for her therapy. Becky introduced me, saying, ''This is my new mommy. I been adopted!''

The visits to Children's helped me get things into perspective. I'd ask myself, *Becky's so much more involved than Julie; can I really handle this?* Then I'd see children so much worse than Becky and realize how very fortunate we were.

I saw children with cerebral palsy who would never walk or talk; I saw kids with brain injuries who were vegetables; I saw children who would always wear cumbersome leg braces; I saw mothers who had breakdowns, fathers who had left, marriages that had been destroyed; and I humbly thanked God for strengthening and protecting us.

When Becky joined our family, there was very little she could do for herself. She was toilet trained, but that meant she would yell, ''I hafta go!'' and then I would carry her into the bathroom, hold her up with one hand, pull her panties down with the other, set her on the toilet, hold her so she wouldn't fall off—or in—and then when she finished we would reverse the whole procedure.

Many times I'd pray for divine wisdom and God would show me how to apply common sense. I borrowed a variety of potty chairs to see which would work best for Becky. Her sitting balance was so poor that if the chair wasn't sturdy enough, she would tip the whole thing over. After experimenting, I went out and bought the broadest based, sturdiest chair made.

''Mommy! I hafta go potty! Take me!''

''Becky, there's your very own potty chair. Take yourself!''

As I watched Becky struggle to pull down her panties and sit, I literally had to sit on my hands to keep from helping her. It would have been much easier and faster to do it myself, but so unfair to Becky.

Becky glared at me while she struggled with a full bladder and an uncooperative body. She kept yelling, ''I'm gonna wet! I'm gonna wet!'' and I thought for sure the bladder would win.

But she made it! And here we were, grown lady and a little black girl, hollering and crying, celebrating in the bathroom. Once I determined that Becky was safe, I made a point of leaving the room while she toileted herself. It was too hard for me to continually watch her painful, torturous struggles.

A friend was visiting that week and it was potty time for Becky. We repeated the conversation. ''Mommy! Mommy! I hafta go!''

''Then go!'' I said, and left her. My friend watched Becky struggling alone, saw me pointedly ignoring Becky, and asked, ''How can you be so hard?''

Hard?

Every battle that we've won, every triumph, every accomplishment, has followed a routine. I would observe what Becky could do, check her out, and then when she seemed ready I would start:

''Becky try this...'' (going potty, getting dressed, tying shoes, etc.).

''But I can't!''

''Becky, you have to try.''

Becky would glare at me, suck that thumb, and eventually try. She would succeed. We would celebrate. She would add one more accomplishment to her growing repertoire. Then we would start again.

One day when Becky was glaring at me I thought, *She hates me!* and I wrote in my journal, ''I'm afraid that I might have to choose between having a helpless, dependent cripple love me, or have a competent, independent person hate me. I hope I can have both, but if I have to choose—I'll have to opt for independence.''

About the time we would win one physical battle we would be faced with solving an emotional one.

"Mommy! Mommy!" Becky's screams would pierce the air. Heart pounding, fears growing, I'd run into her room, expecting at the very least to find King Kong bursting through her window.

"Mommy, I'm awake now. Get me up!"

Becky couldn't get out of bed by herself and couldn't stand to be left alone, so for weeks we repeated that routine. She would scream. I would run. She would yell, "Get me up!" Those screams were her assurance of not being in that room alone any longer than necessary.

The day arrived when I was on a ladder, painting the kitchen ceiling. My arms, back, and neck were aching from the twisted position, and I was splattered with wet paint.

Becky screamed. I got down from my paint-speckled perch and ran into her room. "What's wrong?" (I'm obviously a slow learner.)

"I'm awake. Get me up!"

"Get yourself up," I snapped.

Becky looked at me and glared. Stuck that thumb in her mouth. Looked down at the chasm between her and the floor. Looked imploringly at me. Got no result. Glared again. Then she tossed off her covers and slowly, arduously, triumphantly got out of bed.

And then there were the slamming doors. With a windy city, lots of doors, and three committed door slammers, we had a problem. Every time a door slammed she would startle and scream. We tried blocking the doors open and warning the kids and their friends, but it was impossible.

Slam!

"Why are you screaming, Becky?"

"The door slammed," she would sniffle.

"Well, why don't you slam it back?"

I had her slam the door. Instant hysterics. We slammed it again. She was a little quieter. Once Becky could finally slam the door without screaming, I showed her how to open it and we had another monster licked.

Every time that I've wanted that divine wisdom, the wisdom of Solomon (or at least a degree in child psychology), and I've berated my lack of experience and expertise, I've been humbly reminded of 1 Corinthians 1:29 and how God purposefully uses the foolish and simple "so that no one anywhere can ever brag in the presence of God."

Then there was food. Becky had been a preemie and in an early placement was fed milk and junk food; she was fairly immobile and not burning off many calories; and I'm certain there was a big difference between my cooking habits and those of her foster mother. All this combined for one giant eating problem.

Breakfast was fine—if I'd stick to cereal or waffles. (I'd quickly learned that eggs were a disaster.) One chilly fall morning I did my "super Mommy" routine and fixed hot cereal.

Becky looked in her bowl, glared at me, pushed the bowl away, and declared, "My foster mother never made me eat this!" We learned that you can't *make* a child eat. Becky would close her mouth, push the bowl away, and if all else failed she would gag.

Finally she wised up. "This is delicious, Mommy. I just love it. You're the bestest cook ever. Oh, boy, is this good." With exaggerated motions she would chew and chew, stopping only long enough to pass out more compliments. When it was time to clear the table, I would discover that she hadn't eaten a bite.

I had learned all the proper lessons with the first three about the futility of force feeding. I *knew* it didn't work. I *knew* it caused problems. I *knew* that as long as the food was there she wouldn't starve. I *knew*....

But it seemed that all of the adoption agency, the state of California, the courts, and the social workers were hovering in our kitchen—crowded place!—waiting to pounce on me and grab Becky away. "Aha! You starved her!"

The children each have a night to say grace, and when it was Becky's turn she would try a new ploy: "Dear God, thank You for the vegetables [which she hates], thank You for the farmers that grow them, thank You for the rain You send, for the fertilizer, for the ...." Poor child thought that if she prayed long enough and hard enough, dinner would be over.

Adopting for the first time is like having that first child over again, and repeating all those same mistakes, and making a few new ones.

I had some fantasies to get rid of, and without realizing it I was expecting Becky to be brimming with gratitude whenever we gave her anything. Instead she would say, "A red dress? I wanted blue!"

In the foster home, the mother *took care* of Becky and the father *cared for* her. Becky expected this to continue. "Daddy, can I have a hug?" "Mommy, wipe my nose!"

Becky was and is her own unique, wonderful, complex self, not a perfect fantasy child.

Those first months were exhausting, my back was killing me, my nerves were often frayed, and many days I'd yell, *Hey, God! Remember You promised—no more than I can handle.*

He would take me in His arms, give me a godly love, pat me on the back, give me a "pep talk" from His Word, and rested and strengthened I would go on.

Those first months weren't all bad times and frayed nerves. There were many triumphs and joys mingled in.

Becky hadn't been to church before, and she absorbed the experience like a thirsty little sponge. She would go around the house singing at the top of her lungs, "Jesus loves me, this I know."

There was one unforgettable bedtime after a really rotten day. Becky had her nightgown on, and I turned out the light and started to tuck her in. She wasted no time starting her prayers. "Dear God, don't believe a thing my mother tells you."

Then there was the ultimate compliment: Becky gave me a big hug and whispered, "You're the bestest mommy *I ever had.*"

Much as Becky idolized Dennis, we were both superfluous. She loved the kids, and Julie was her heroine:

"Julie wears bigger braces than me and she walks. One day I'll walk."

"Julie roller skates and rides a bike. I will, too."

Julie told us, "I really think I know why God made me this way—so I can help and encourage Becky."

We had the elders pray for Becky and Julie for physical healing. The next night we found Julie playing a strange game with her new sister.

Julie would stand Becky up, then let go. Becky would fall flat on her face. Julie would pick her up, stand her up again, and splat!

"Julie, what are you doing?"

"We prayed for God to heal Becky, and we're just trying to see if He has yet."

By the end of October, our brief "honeymoon" period was over. The social workers usually recommend that the kids not see their former foster parents for at least six months. Before that it can be too confusing. In October we met the foster mother for a previously made appointment with Becky's eye surgeon.

That night as I tucked Becky in and kissed her good night, she looked at me and declared, "I wanna go back to my old parents." I kept telling myself, *I'm a mature, logical adult.* I was crushed.

"Becky, we love you very much. We prayed for God to send us a special little girl and He did. Your home now is with us. Your foster family loved you, but their job is caring for babies until they get adopted. They don't keep the kids and you can't go back.''

Our talk seemed to help. However, later that week, whenever she would get mad at Julie, Becky would threaten, "If you don't give me that dolly...If you don't play with me...I'll go back." Then Julie would cry.

Later that afternoon Becky asked me for a cookie.

"No, honey. It's too close to dinner."

"If you don't give me a cookie—right now!—I'll go back to my foster parents."

"Becky, we all love you very much. We all want you to live with us, but if that's what you really want, I'll call your social worker. Here is a paper bag, start packing.''(This is *not* recommended procedure.)

Trying to show a calm I definitely wasn't feeling, I went to the phone, dialed T-I-M-E, and held an imaginary conversation. "Hello, this is Bonnie Wheeler.''

"Hang up! Hang up! I really wanna stay!'' Becky screamed. I put down the phone, we put the bags away, and I gave her a big hug and said, "I'm so very glad you want to stay.''

She never made that threat again, but it later hit me: *Dear God, what would I have done if she'd called my bluff?*

One of the hardest things with special children is finding just the right medical and support services. We found a terrific pediatric clinic, and Dr. Remo Cerruti became Becky's pediatrician. Becky was absolutely terrified of doctors and would stiffen up so much that it was almost impossible for him to examine her. But Dr. Cerruti has an abundance of patience and never got short-tempered with her.

We saw the doctor often that first year; Dr. Cerruti likes to keep a close watch on his special kids, and he wanted to build up Becky's confidence. No matter how busy he was, there was always time for Becky's hugs and kisses. There was always time to ask, "How is it going? Any problems? Any questions?'' And he'd really listen. After a few months Becky was relaxed, cooperative, and in love.

Becky had an unfortunate experience with an impatient dentist and really balked at another visit. We heard of a Christian dentist and I told Becky about him. ''I'll try,'' she reluctantly consented.

''Hi! My mommy says you are a Christian?''

''That's right, Becky,'' he answered.

''You *really* love Jesus?'' Becky the skeptic asked.

''Yes, Becky. I *really* do.''

''OK, I'll open my mouth.''

There were—and still are—many aspects of Becky that I don't understand and no one has been able to explain to me. Her biological mother had a drug problem, and what this did to the developing fetus is a mystery. The little information I've been able to find points out that these children often show a higher rate of unexplainable emotional highs and lows.

We were able to see God's hand in our crisis center experience and the resultant peace God gave us in dealing with the unexplainable side of Becky.

At times I'll grow frustrated with my lack of knowledge, with my inability to cope, and I'll remember all the reassurances God has given us that ''Becky is just exactly the child I want you to have.''

I'll pray, *Lord, I'm at a loss. I don't know what to do. You'll have to take care of this, please.*

And He always does.

In February we were told about the parents' group that was run by the adoption agency. These ''rap'' sessions are held for parents adopting older children. The social workers were excellent and assured us that we could be as open as necessary and that ''nothing will be used against you.''

Many of the adjustment problems we were having with

Becky were typical of these adopted children. The worker explained, "So many more families are adopting older children, and we discovered a need for these groups to help parents cope with problems that never occurred in the days of infant adoptions."

The group was a mixture of couples considering adoption, couples who had just had a child placed with them, and couples back for another child.

It was a tremendous help to hear someone else describe a problem we were having as "part of the adjustment process, not a permanent part of the child's personality."

"All of these children go through a mourning process," the social worker explained. We all looked surprised and the worker continued, "No matter how bad or good their past home was, these kids still go through a time of mourning with its sense of loss and rejection. And they all go through certain stages:

"'If I'm bad these new people will send me away.'

"'If I'd been really good my foster parents would have kept me.'

"'I thought they loved me; how could they send me away?'

"'I hate them for sending me away.'

"'I hate my new family for taking me away.'

"'I must be a very bad person for my biological parents to not want me.'

"All of these conflicting emotions show up in these kids," she continued. "The mourning process takes almost a year and, of course, varies from child to child. But it does eventually end!"

There were days when it seemed Becky had a written list of the house rules and very methodically went down the list and broke them all. I'd reach the point where I was ready to tear my hair out with frustration at the constant disobedience and my inability to deal effectively with it. Uncannily, that next week's group would cover our problem: "These kids will go through a time of testing to see just how bad they can be before they're rejected by you, too."

With this new insight I was able, the next time Becky went down her list, to give her a big hug and say, "I don't like what you're doing, but I sure love you, and nothing you can ever do will make us send you away."

The Lord has been with us each and every step of the way. Always providing just what we need. Just when we need it. The adoptive parents' group was one of the many times He's already had a solution for us, often before we've even identified the problem.

I am so grateful that God is so much more patient than I am. There were many times when I was feeling frustrated at the seeming lack of progress we were making with Becky. During one of these periods I sat down and wrote out a list of all the problems Becky had when she first arrived: falls constantly when sitting; screams when left alone; screams at slamming doors; completely dependent on others.

After I finished the list I went back over it and updated it: still falls over; no longer screams at slamming doors; doesn't like being left alone but has stopped screaming about it; can get out of bed and toilet herself now.

When I reviewed the two lists, I was delighted at the many improvements that had been made. After I prayed and thanked God for showing me the progress, I had a very humbling thought: *If God made out a similar list for me, how many improvements would I show?*

Becky graduated from her walker to crutches but was having trouble getting the timing right. Dennis would spread books down the hall and set up an obstacle course for her, and they would make a game out of it. "Left foot, right crutch. Right foot, left crutch."

The payoff came the day she was able to use the crutches for church. The children were all waiting in the car when Becky came out. Since nothing of Becky's works automatically, she really had to concentrate for each move. Becky slowly walked down the driveway and fearfully looked at the curb.

"Come on, Becky!"

"You can do it!"

"Come on, Becky!"

Slowly, hesitantly, triumphantly she did.

In November Becky started preschool at Glankler School for the Orthopedically Handicapped. I stayed in the room while the psychologist tested her, and after forty-five minutes Becky was obviously growing tired.

"Now tell me what shape this is," the doctor asked.

Becky looked at him, looked at his latest shape, looked back at him, and said, "I'm tired. You tell me what shape it is!"

My first impression of Glankler was its friendliness. There were wide halls and doorways to accommodate the wheelchairs; the walls had bright posters on them; and the staff members seemed handpicked for their warmth and friendliness.

Becky would be receiving physical therapy and occupational therapy during the school day, and our weekly trips to Oakland came to an end. The district even provided transportation for her to Glankler.

Becky's teacher had read all her records and was delightfully surprised when she met the real child. "We had expected a basket case," she said. We maintained close contact, much to Becky's dismay:

"When do you think she'll be able to toilet herself," the teacher would ask.

"She's been doing that for ages."

"Oh!"

"The other day when I was putting on her coat for her—" I told the teacher.

"Mrs. Wheeler, she's been doing that for weeks."

"Oh?"

"Becky!"

At the same time Becky was starting school, my doctor discovered that I had an enlarged thyroid, and I was put on medication to try to either shrink it or control it. I was still having arthritic side effects from my bout with the measles, and I'd had a chronic sinus infection for over a year. What I feared was a reaction to the adoption turned out to be my body's inability to handle the thyroid medication. I changed doctors, was taken off the medication, and my specialist ordered sinus surgery.

I was deeply puzzled about why I was having so many health problems when I knew the Lord wanted us to have Becky and I needed all the physical and emotional strength I could muster.

In 2 Corinthians 12:9 I came across Paul's words:

> Now I am glad to boast about how weak I am;
> I am glad to be a living demonstration
> of Christ's power, instead of showing
> off my own power and abilities.

That first Christmas with Becky was a mixture of blessings. There were so many presents that we hardly knew where to start, and we were all eager to watch Becky's excitement. She opened two presents and keeled over.

I called Dr. Cerruti and described her symptoms. "Sounds like she has a virus and this is her reaction. Just let her sleep it off," he said. We eventually discovered that this was part of Becky's cerebral palsy pattern and that whenever she got excited or overtired she'd have an attack of her sleeping sickness.

Christmas afternoon, Becky started feeling better and she gave us our gift. *A typical kid's gift,* I thought as I saw a plaque covered with macaroni and spray-painted gold. I started reading the poem on the plaque to Dennis, got halfway through, and couldn't finish. It was by no means a "typical" present, and the poem has become one of our treasures.

Heaven's Very Special Child
A meeting was held quite far from earth,
"It's time again for another birth"
Said the Angels to the Lord above.
"This Special Child will need much love.

His progress may be very slow,
Accomplishments he may not show.
And he'll require extra care
From the folks he meets down there.

He may not run or laugh or play;
His thoughts may seem quite far away.
In many ways he won't adapt
And he'll be known as handicapped.

So let's be careful where he's sent.
We want his life to be content.
Please Lord find the parents who
Will do a special job for You.

They will not realize right away
The leading role they're asked to play.
But with this child sent from above
Comes stronger faith and richer love.

And soon they'll know the privilege given
In caring for their gift from Heaven.
Their precious charge so meek and mild
Is Heaven's Very Special Child."*

*This is part of "This is Our Life," by John and Edna Massimilla, P.O. Box 21, Hatboro, PA 19040. Copyright 1956. Printed with permission.

In March 1975, we had a Japanese exchange student living with us. Junko was a delight and loved the children. Wynn and C.B. Stack had a Japanese boy, Yasiuki, staying with them, and we were able to do many things together.

Robby is a terrible tease, and he quickly discovered that Junko and Yasiuki didn't like being called Chinese. Robby would run up to Junko, shout "You Chinese"; then she would run after him. They would run all around the house, and when Junko finally caught Robby she would tickle him and ask, "What am I Robby? What am I?" When Robby couldn't stand being tickled any longer he would gasp, "You Japanese," and the game would end.

We visited a huge shopping mall one day, and Robby decided to try his game with Yasiuki. Yasiuki calmly picked up the feisty little kid and held him out over the railing, letting Robby get a good look down. "What I, Robby?" he asked with Oriental cool. *"Japanese,"* yelled Robby—clear, loud, and quick.

In early 1976 a group was started at Glankler that was similar to the one sponsored by the adoption agency. This group was led by the psychologist and one of the therapists. We had always treated Julie like any other child and had been dealing with Becky the same way.

As we compared notes on our children's behavior, I discovered that there were many similarities in these physically challenged children. During one session I heard a couple complain about the way they'd been manipulated by their child. I interrupted with, "I dont't believe what I'm hearing. That's not four-year-old behavior."

The psychologist explained, "These kids start therapy when they're a few months old, and they're around a constant stream of adults. They start school at three, and in many ways they seem to have more mature behavior patterns.''

Another week someone complained, "Boy! Was my daughter sassy today." This had been bothering us about Becky. We've always trained the children to be respectful, and Becky had quickly been nicknamed "Miss Mouth."

"These children are often allowed to talk back," the psychologist said. "They're mauled, manipulated, taken out of class for therapy that's often painful and uncomfortable. They have little control over their bodies and less control over what's done to those bodies. So, yes, they're often mouthy."

"My kid was a brat!" With that comment the floodgates opened. With these special kids, any time we complain about their behavior to friends, neighbors, or, worst of all, relatives, we're asked, "How can you talk that way about a child like this?"

Any child—mobile or not, black, white, or purple—has good days and bad. The parents of these children have a need to voice complaints and comments without being judged. One of the best things anyone can do for the parents of a physically challenged child is listen. Just listen and don't judge.

When Becky joined our family she was three, small, and not very heavy. She was so spastic that it was very difficult to carry her, but she could use a stroller.

Becky learned to use a walker and eventually crutches, but only very slowly and for short distances. When I would start to think about the future Becky, taller and heavier, I'd tend to panic.

"We can't carry her forever," I'd tell Dennis. "They say she won't improve much, and she won't fit in the stroller much longer. Maybe we need a wheelchair."

Whenever I would mention "wheelchair," strange things would happen. In professional circles, *walking* is the ultimate goal. Walking is terrific, but when all the emphasis is on walking—not how well you walk or how you feel when you finally arrive—then those goals need to be reexamined.

For a year I had felt guilty every time I got up enough nerve to mention "wheelchair" to anyone. Becky was getting heavier and increasingly upset on outings, but she couldn't say why. She was still falling often, still not supposed to improve much, if any. But a wheelchair? Horrors!

Then one of the Glankler therapists attended a meeting in which several adults with cerebral palsy spoke:

"All the emphasis was on being upright and walking."

"I spent more time in therapy than in school, yet I'll have to make my way in the world with my brain, not my legs."

"It hurt, I was slow," another of the speakers complained. "I was always late to class, always exhausted when I arrived. By the time I finally got to class, I was too tired to concentrate. As an adult *I* made the decision to use the wheelchair for long distances, and I couldn't believe the difference. It's often inconvenient, but I feel so much better."

The therapist told us, "I think we need to do some reevaluation about those kids who won't be functional walkers."

"What's the definition of a 'functional walker'?" I asked.

"Basically, it's someone who can safely and comfortably go Christmas shopping or walk around the zoo."

"Will Becky ever be a functional walker?"

"No," answered the therapist.

"When Becky has her surgery, she'll be off her feet and in a wheelchair for five months. Can we order her chair and use that as a transition period?" I asked.

The next week Becky was measured and her chair was ordered. I did seriously examine my motives: *Am I giving up? Am I lacking faith? Doubting God?* But after I asked and answered all those questions, I was certain we had made the right decision. In all honesty, I wanted the very best for Becky and saw the use of the wheelchair—at least part of the time—as being part of God's best for Becky. We go to the zoo and she's higher and can see more. When she's in a crowd she doesn't worry about falling and cracking her head. Too much emphasis has been put on *the arrival,* and not enough on "How does she feel when she arrives?"

In God's perfect timing, He used the parents' group at Glankler to help us. First, He showed us those parts of Becky's personality that were a result of her physical problems and frustrations. Second, He prepared us for her coming surgery. We had been told from the start that Becky would have surgery the year she turned five. It had seemed far away then.

For eighteen months we worked, struggled, loved, sweated, and prayed together to give this child some measure of emotional stability and security. I'd constantly trusted the Lord with those problems and He'd always been abundantly faithful, but now I was letting the enormity of the coming surgery get me down.

"Becky's foster mother told us that she (Becky) was so upset after the last eye surgery that she had required medication until September," I said to the doctor. "And she was only in the hospital twelve hours. What will this do to her?"

Dr. Hook told us, "Becky will enter the hospital on Sunday. I'll operate on Monday morning, and she'll be hospitalized about five days.

"I'll lengthen the heel cords," the doctor continued, "take a bone graft from her shin, and use that to repair her collapsed ankles. The heel cord lengthening will help some, but our main concern is those ankles. As she gets heavier and puts more weight on parts of her feet that aren't meant to be weight-bearing, the pain will get so intense that she won't be able to stand or walk at all. The surgery will be more preventative than corrective."

Becky's friend went in for a similar surgery about six weeks before, and her mother discussed the experience with our group. That talk was a great help to those of us whose children had surgeries scheduled because it helped take away the fear of the unknown.

Shortly before Becky entered the hospital, her friend came back to school. Becky was able to see her alive and well. Both legs were in casts but intact.

Becky fearfully asked, "How was it?"

Her friend replied, "It wasn't bad, but the food was rotten!"

I was determined to be honest with Becky about the coming surgery. "Now, honey," I said, "you know this will hurt some—"

"Don't worry, Mommy," she interrupted. "My friend told me all about it. If it hurts, Dr. Hook will just give me a shot."

As the week before Easter approached, my panic grew. I talked about it with the group and asked, "Will this undo all the progress that she's made?"

The therapist looked me in the eye and confidently said, "Forget that! You're not even dealing with the same child now. Becky has so much self-confidence and security now, and nothing can take that away from her."

Lord, here I am again. The time is drawing near, and I'm no help to myself or Becky. I'm scared, and only You can take that fear away. Be with Becky, calm her. Don't let us lose the progress that's been made.

I prayed specifically about the aspects of the surgery: my daily drives to Hayward, Julie's caring for the other kids, and the pressures on us all. Then I added a postscript: *Lord, please help my back. I'm worried about what five months of lifting Becky and casts will do to my already aching back.*

Palm Sunday arrived. We all went to church that morning

and stayed after to have the pastors and the elders pray for Becky. While the men were praying, I opened my eyes to check on Becky. She looked so small and helpless in the big chair; just as her body would sway and she'd start to fall over, one of the gentle hands would steady her. Holding her upright were the loving hands of the men praying for her.

Oh, Lord, how like You that is. Whenever I'm ready to fall, there You are with Your gentle, loving hands to hold me up and keep me from falling. Be with Becky, Lord. Bring about the very best You have for her.

On our way home from church Becky said, "Mommy! Daddy! This morning in Sunday school I asked Jesus into my heart. He's going to the hospital with me."

Dennis and I planned the best way to deal with Becky's hospitalization. We wanted to avoid as much trauma as possible, and I still vividly remembered the fears and insecurities that we had suffered through with Timmy and Robby after their hospitalizations.

I found coloring books, story books, and magic pencil books at the Christian bookstore. We wanted constant reminders for Becky that "even though we're not here, Jesus is." For each day of her hospital stay there was a lollipop taped to a book. "When we've read the last book and you've eaten the last lollipop, you'll be home," we told her.

We packed a pretty new nightgown, the candy, the books, and her favorite doll and left for the hospital. After Becky was all checked in and finished with her tests, Dennis and I told her, "We're going for coffee. We'll be back in a few minutes."

We went for coffee several times that afternoon, just to assure Becky that when we would say, "We'll be back," she could believe us.

When visiting hours ended we prayed together, "Dear Jesus, stay with Becky while she's here." We kissed her good night and promised, "See you early tomorrow morning."

At 7 A.M. Dennis and I walked down the corridor, cautiously listening for Becky's screams. Dennis turned to me and said, "I hear her already. Do you?"

Becky's voice was loud and shrill. Her squeals and giggles filled the hallway. Becky was having her pre-op bath and loving it. "Hi, Daddy! Hi, Mommy! I slept all night and now I'm having a bubble bath."

Dennis had to leave for work, and I read to Becky until they took her off to the operating room. Then I waited four hours. I had taken a book with me, but the words made no sense. Mostly I prayed and was grateful that God understands and knows our prayers even when we're incoherent.

Finally! The long wait was over. Dr. Hook sank onto the sofa, and he looked exhausted. "Everything went well. She's in recovery. Our concern now is that the bone graft 'takes.' A certain amount of these don't and have to be done again."

I couldn't see Becky for another hour, so I called Dennis and the children, had a cup of coffee, and took a long walk before I returned to Becky's room.

In the middle of this enormous white bed was this tiny black body with two huge, white plaster casts all the way up her thighs. Becky looked so frail, pitiful and—longer? *Why longer?* I asked myself. Then I realized it was the first time I'd ever seen Becky's legs straight, and she was inches longer.

As Becky started to come out of the anesthetic, her crying was pathetic; she was in a lot of pain; then she started gagging. "Nurse! Nurse!" I pressed the call button repeatedly and yelled. No one came. I was terrified that Becky would aspirate and was equally scared to sit her up. When I saw that help wasn't coming, I forced myself to calm down, turned her head to the side, cleaned up around her, got a tray, and waited for the next time.

Fifteen minutes later the nurse arrived. "I was busy with

another patient and I knew you were here," she said.

I was wild.

Much has been studied and written about the magic of "bonding" between mother and child shortly after birth. Becky and I had our bonding experience that afternoon. That day I became Becky's mother. She wasn't black. I wasn't white. She wasn't adopted. Basic, primitive mother instincts took over. "This is my child," said Momma Lion. "I will protect her, I will fight for her." The next four hours I stayed by Becky's bed. I was afraid to leave her even briefly. Off and on, all afternoon she would gag. She was so weak she couldn't even turn her head to vomit, much less call for help. So I stayed.

They moved three babies into the room and, being babies, they cried. Every time they cried Becky would wake up, hurting and moaning. Momma Lion would try to get the nurse to "Please quiet those babies."

Four hours I sat and protected *my* child. As I gazed at her, tears filled my eyes. *My God! I love her! She's my child and I love her!*

There were so many struggles during those early days of our mutual adjusting that it was easy for me to lose sight of the child. I knew we were doing God's will; I knew I was committed to the *cause;* but what about the child? People constantly ask, "Can you really love an adopted child like your own?" On bad days I'd remember their words and wonder, *Can I? Do I?*

During that long, long day those doubts went away. I knew that there would still be problems and adjustments (we'll never be able to completely undo all the trauma of Becky's first three years). But the day of her surgery we cut down any color barriers, any biological barriers, any physical barriers. *She's my child. I'm her mother. And on that basis we'll fight and conquer whatever the future holds.*

By evening Becky's nausea had finally subsided. She was still sleeping fitfully, and her pain was much worse. Momma Lion roared one more time. The doctor was phoned and extra medication was ordered. My vigil was ended.

Tuesday morning when I arrived at the hospital, Becky had a slight fever. She moaned a lot, didn't want to eat, hated the bedpan, and didn't notice her flowers.

Wednesday morning I arrived and walked past the nurses' station. The nurses started laughing and told me, "There's a surprise waiting for you."

Puzzled and curious, I hurried down to Becky's room. Her hair was fluffed out, she was sitting up, and a big smile lit up her face when she saw me. "Surprise, Mommy! I get to go home today."

I couldn't believe what I was seeing or hearing. Then the nurse entered the room. "When Dr. Hook made rounds this morning, Becky's fever was down," the nurse said. "Becky looked at the doctor and said, 'I need to go home. My mommy's awfully worried about me.'"

I ran down to sign Becky out and get her medication. When I returned there were *two* nurses trying to get Becky into the wheelchair. "Good grief!" I said. "If it takes two of you to get her in that, how will I manage when I get her home?"

My elation was disappearing as I considered all the practicalities involved. *How can I keep her on the seat? She can't sit up and the seat belt won't work with her lying down. We haven't picked up our wheelchair yet, and I don't even have the bedpan. Lord, help!*

As I uttered that short but heartfelt prayer, I literally bumped into the answer. Wynn and C.B. had just arrived to visit Becky. Instead of the planned visit, they helped me get Becky home. The nurses put Becky in the car, and Wynn sat next to her to keep her from falling. When we arrived home,

C.B. gently carried Becky inside to the excited shouts of "Becky's home! Becky's home!"

After Becky was settled in, Wynn and C.B. picked up Becky's wheelchair. Here was another example of God's perfect timing, answered prayer, and practical Christianity.

Becky is normally a little dictator, and we were concerned about what being totally dependent on others would do. But she was terrific. Becky trained her little brother to run and get Dennis or me when she had to use the bathroom. After the first month her legs were x-rayed, and the heavy casts were replaced with knee-length, lighter casts. She could sit up, was lighter to carry, and hygiene was much easier.

I learned an important lesson during Becky's convalesence: here was this houseful of children inventing new excuses to get out of their chores, and the totally dependent Becky was begging for work. She wanted—and needed—to help and contribute to the family. We tried to come up with jobs she could safely do.

Every Saturday morning Becky would holler, "I have work to do, put me down!" I'd get a wet sponge and lay it on the hearth. Then I would put Becky on the floor and she would scoot herself along with her arms. She would wipe every speck of dust off the hearth and clean the television screen.

We would pick her up and put her back on the sofa to rest. She was very tired, but a helping member of the family.

Becky's main complaints were almost comical: one of her friends asked how the hospital was and Becky told her, "The food is awful, and they take your panties away and your buns get cold!"

Becky wore her casts all through the summer and would often call, "Mommy, there's a fly in my cast!"

"Becky, there can't be a fly in your cast."

"But Mommy, there hasta be. It itches!"

When Becky started back to school, I asked her therapist if

she had noticed an improvement in Becky's sitting balance.

"Yes, I noticed. But I think it's just a reaction to the casting. She'll probably start tipping over again when they're removed."

After five months the casts were removed, and we watched Becky sit, unsupported and not falling over. Her sitting balance remains 90 percent improved. The Lord so generously answered our prayers during that time, and I didn't have a single backache until the week *after* the casts were removed.

After Becky's casts were removed in September, there were months of therapy and exercise. We were into the early months of 1977 when Julie called us into the family room:

"Hey! Watch this! Becky has a surprise for you."

We all crowded into the family room. "Well, come on! Where's the big surprise?" Dennis said.

Becky stood by the sofa.

Becky slowly balanced herself.

She took her hand off the supporting sofa and slowly, cautiously, but unaided and unsupported, Becky *walked* across the family room.

As the whole family whooped and hollered and celebrated, Becky gave us all a saucy grin, as if to say, "I sure showed them doctors, didn't I?"

After many conferences and much discussion, the staff at Glankler decided Becky was ready for her next big step. In September 1977, she would start first grade at our neighborhood school.

During Becky's first week at the neighborhood school, I drove her. The first few days I took her right to her class, but then each succeeding day I had her go farther by herself.

Robby was a big help to Becky, and they have a typical sibling relationship—allies one day, enemies the next. Robby would meet Becky at the bus and take her to class; he would protect her at recess; help her at lunch; then take her back to the bus in the afternoon.

During one recess Robby and Becky were having one of their arguments, and an irate teacher came up, glared at Robby, and yelled, "You stop picking on her!"

Robby defensively replied, "Aw, I can pick on *her*. She's my sister."

The male teacher looked at black Becky, looked at freckled Robby, and retorted, "Yeah, and I'm your grandmother!"

Before Becky's first day at the new school, there was a meeting of the admissions and dismissal board at which the experts reviewed her record; her teacher, therapists, and the principal all gave their opinions.

Two therapists then toured the school with Becky. All the doors were measured; the desks were checked out; and the cafeteria and bathrooms were examined for safety and accessibility. A meeting was held with her new teacher. After I left Becky at school that first morning, all the rest of the day my thoughts were racing:

What if she falls? Will the other kids like her? What if they tease her? Maybe we all made a mistake.

With myriad questions flooding my head, I met Becky after school and fearfully asked, "How was your day?"

Becky flashed her big, front-teeth-missing smile and answered, "It was great! I made lots of new friends, got a birthday party invitation, love my teacher, and tomorrow I want peanut butter."

7
Benji

IN EARLY 1975 we told our social worker, "We would like you to watch for another child for us. We think Becky's overall adjustment will be easier if she's not the only adopted child in our family, and we really just want another child. We'd like a little girl, younger than Becky, with a slight handicap and preferably non-Caucasian."

"Well, I think you're both gluttons," she said, "but I'll look around."

On her next visit, the worker told us of another child under her care: "I didn't think of this child last time because you had asked for a girl. There's this little boy who is fourteen months old. He's black and Mexican and has mild cerebral palsy. Would you consider him?"

The medical dossier was hardly encouraging: cerebral palsy (our speciality), retarded, respiratory and digestive problems. "The doctor diagnosed him as retarded because he slept most of the first year," our social worker explained.

I turned to Dennis and said, "He certainly sounds needy, but?..."

"I know how you feel," Dennis replied. "Is it fair to take on such an involved child with the four we already have?"

Our conversation would have continued, but the worker laid out some pictures on the table. All talking ceased as I grabbed those photos. Tears filled my eyes and I again turned to Dennis. "Look! Isn't he beautiful? Look at that smile. Oh, Dennis?"

Dennis looked at the picture, gave a knowing smile, and asked the social worker, "When can we see him?" We were supposedly mature, intelligent adults, but it was clearly a case of love at first sight.

I had a preliminary telephone conversation with the foster mother, and that evening Dennis and I discussed the baby. The gist of our conclusion was: "The Lord has just had him waiting for us. If he was classified as 'normal,' we would never have had a chance, because infants are at such an adoption premium."

The night for our first visit arrived, and we ran through the rain, rang the doorbell, and waited. A tall lady opened the door. "You must be the Wheelers," she said in warm greeting as she ushered us in. She was holding the most beautiful child I had ever seen. His skin was so many hues of brown, gold, and tan that it was indescribably gorgeous; he had a crop of hair that looked like a fluffy halo; and he wore a smile that lit up that dark, damp night. And his eyes—they were dark, beautiful, enormous eyes, fringed with thick long lashes that would be the envy of any beauty queen.

I automatically put out my arms, and he came right to me. The mystified foster mother kept saying, "He's never done that before. He never goes to strangers. Never. I just don't understand."

I had to bite back my reply: "I'm no stranger. I'm his mother."

We played with him, learned more of his history, and kept him up past his bedtime. We had brought a toy for him, and he spent the evening playing with it and Dennis. The baby would throw the toy down, have Dennis put him on the carpet, pick up his toy, and beg to be picked up again. Then he'd repeat the whole procedure. We were both captivated.

Smitten. We knew he needed to go to bed so we finally, reluctantly, left.

I was scheduled for sinus surgery on April 10, and we knew that any plans for another child would have to wait until I had recovered (and after seeing the baby I was determined to have a very speedy recovery).

We made an appointment to bring the children out to see the baby on Sunday, then started the drive home. "Isn't he beautiful?" I said to Dennis. "I can hardly wait to see him again."

We bombarded each other with questions and believed that he was the second child God had specifically picked out for us. We had both forgotten that we had ever asked for another girl. He was exactly what we wanted. We would name him Benjamin Joel.

We listened as the social worker and his foster mother went over Benji's official diagnosis and prognosis:

cerebral palsy: "This is the reason for his slow motor development and why he's just now starting to sit up and crawl."

retarded: "This is because he slept most of his first year."

emotional problems: "He's very withdrawn and doesn't respond to strangers."

breathing problems: "Chronic congestion."

digestive trouble: "He'll only tolerate the most strained baby foods."

Common sense—and most of our friends—said, "This is too much!" But we had fallen for a smile, big brown eyes, and God's will.

However, we did honestly ask ourselves, "What if the doctors are right? Could we deal with all that?" We would read a few more promises from God's Word, visit Benji again, and become convinced, "No matter what Benji's future holds, we want to be part of it."

Once again I turned to my Bible for guidance, and I read in Exodus how God led His people out of Egypt. When they came to the sea God told Moses, "Quit praying and get the people moving! Forward, march!" (Exodus 14:15).

Lord, give us the faith of Moses. When he saw those doubting Israelites behind him and the raging sea before him and You said, "March!" Moses had to step out in faith, trusting You to keep Your word, part the waters, and lead them all to safety. Give us that kind of faith as we take this child into our family. Part the waters for Benji, Lord. Lead him on to health and happiness.

We stepped out in faith, not knowing if our next step would be in the water or on dry ground, but knowing that it would be far better to be "in the water" with the Lord than to settle for the "dry ground" without Him.

We went with the children that weekend to let them meet Benji. Becky popped her thumb in her mouth, stared at the black and beautiful Benji, thought the whole situation over, and then gave her benediction: "He looks just like me!"

Benji wrestled with Timmy, played ball with Robby, and climbed off and on Dennis's lap. When Benji got tired, he would scoot across to Julie for a cuddle. He was an instant success.

The children shouted questions all the way home:

"When do we get him?"

"When can he move in?"

"Can he sleep in my room?"

"When's our next visit?"

Dennis tried to sort out their questions and added, "We'll see him again this next week. And we'll have to wait until after Mom's surgery for Benji to move in."

When we had visited Becky in her foster home and left her to return to our house, I had felt that we were using that time and preparation for the long haul ahead. With Benji it was much simpler. We just wanted him.

The next week we went for another visit, and Benji spent most of the visit playing with Timmy. Benji would hit Timmy, and Timmy would make a big production of falling over. Benji would laugh and clap his pudgy little hands.

I had never been alone with Benji, and I wanted to see how he would react to leaving with me. I put his jacket on him and we went for a walk. The day was windy, and after a very brief walk I took him to the car for a few minutes alone.

We are often asked, "Can you really love an adopted child as much as one you've given birth to?" Those first moments alone with Benji, sitting in the otherwise empty car, were every bit as special as similar times with the first three children. I held Benji tight, sang "Jesus loves you," gave him a big kiss, and said for the first time—and definitely not the last—"Benji, my son, I love you."

When we started telling friends that we were, again, adding to our family, they were incredulous. "You have more than enough to handle already," they said. "Enough's enough!"

Angrily I wrote in my journal, "If I would take the time and money that we would be investing in Benji and use them to go to college, we would be applauded. But to take that same time, money, and energy and invest it in a child—we're told, 'You're nuts!'"

While we were waiting for Benji to join our family, I was praying daily for God's guidance. As much as we already loved and wanted Benji, we wanted God's will even more.

In my Bible reading one day, there was Matthew 18:5:

> And any of you who welcomes
> a little child like this
> because you are mine, is
> welcoming me and caring for me.

I claimed that verse for Benji, and a few weeks later, when I had read my way to Luke 9:48, there was God's reaffirmation:

> Anyone who takes care of
> a little child like this
> is caring for me!

I use a small devotional, *Our Daily Bread,* and I have this bad habit of reading ahead. One devotion was so special that I have it taped in the back of my Bible. Once again there was the verse from Matthew 18:5; there was the poem "Heaven's Special Child"; and there was a little poem by Henry Bosch:

> If there has come into your home
> A babe that needs much special care,
> Receive with love that little one
> As if God sent the Christ child there.

We have as a Good Friday tradition at our church that we take communion in individual family groups. That Good Friday of 1975, C.B. Stack served the sacraments to our family and prayed: "God, bless the little one soon to join their family. Work out the details and smooth the way for his adoption into the Wheeler family and into Your family."

Benji's foster family brought him to our home for a visit the week before Easter, and we gave him a blue rabbit appropriately named Benjamin Bunny. Benji would play with his namesake and then scurry off to find the boys. When he grew tired of playing, he would come to me and lift his little arms for me to pick him up. And I always did.

In all of our preadoptive visits, Benji would always come to me when he was tired, hurt, or just wanted to cuddle. His foster mother was a warm, loving person, and I saw Benji's choosing me as a further sign of God's hand in preparing Benji's heart for us.

During one of our early visits, the foster mother informed me that she would buy Benji a new outfit to wear when he moved to our house. No clothes, no diapers, no toys. After she left I wrote in my prayer journal, "Lord, do I have a prayer request for You." I listed everything we would need for Benji, from diaper pins to a crib. Over the next month it was amazing to watch the Lord supply our every need. We received numerous phone calls in which the caller said, ''I hear you're getting a toddler, and I have some clothes that I've been saving.'' All the perfect size.

We brought a portable crib into Becky's room and rearranged the room for her and Benji to share. When he was older we could move him into the boys' room.

Benji's foster mother brought him into our home, and after a cup of coffee she went shopping. That ''left alone'' visit was special. Benji played with the children, then grew tired and came looking for me. He lifted those dimpled brown arms in an appeal I couldn't resist. I picked him up, got his bottle, and headed for the rocker. Benji snuggled close and went to sleep.

Dear Lord, this is the fifth child I've sat here rocking, and the joy I feel at holding this trusting, sleeping child hasn't diminished since I first held the slumbering Julie. I really don't understand it, Lord. But I thank You for that joy.

Benji came to spend the night and had a good chance to get better acquainted with the children. He liked them all but seemed more comfortable on a one-to-one basis. After dinner, he started fussing and felt warm. He was running a slight temperature and hated the cool bath I gave him. We rocked most of the night.

Benji had a cold. He was teething and miserable, but it gave us a good chance to see how we would work under less-than-perfect circumstances.

On the return trip to the foster home, I drove and Dennis held Benji. Dennis would kiss him on the forehead and Benji would chuckle, cuddle closer, and raise his head for another kiss.

I was scheduled for surgery April 10 and had everything arranged in advance. When I went in for my pre-op exam, my surgeon was concerned about my thyroid condition and decided to postpone the surgery until after I had seen another specialist.

I called Dennis at work and told him, "Hey, I got a reprieve!"

Then I called our social worker. "My surgery is postponed," I told her. "Can we get Benji this weekend?"

She laughed and promised, "I'll call and see if we can arrange that."

Friday afternoon, instead of recovering from surgery, we "had a baby." Benji's foster mother fed him lunch one last time while we signed the placement papers.

That evening Pastor Jeske called and asked, "Dennis, how did Bonnie's surgery go?"

"Well, Pastor, they postponed the surgery, so we got the baby instead."

Pastor laughed and said, "That sounds like Bonnie!"

The children were all enchanted with their new brother, and Benji was very responsive to them. Whenever he would laugh, the kids thought they had received a very special present.

In the evening, when Dennis returned from work, Benji would laugh, giggle, and clap those little hands with pure joy—"Daddy's home!"

I took Benji for a ride one of those first days, and he loved it. When we returned home and pulled into the driveway, Benji saw the front door, recognized it, clapped his hands, and laughed. Benji Wheeler was home.

That first Saturday we wanted to show off our new son, so we took him to the shoe store to get a pair of white high tops. The salesman was friendly and very interested. "I thought it was rough to adopt these days," he said. There was a slight pause before he added, "But I guess ones *like him* are easier to get." Dennis and I bit our tongues, exerted all our self-control, and took our considerable shoe business elsewhere.

Becky started school six weeks after she moved in, and I used that time to run errands and do the shopping. Usually when I was out with Becky, Dennis was with me.

I made an interesting discovery with Benji: lots of stares, glares, and strange looks—when we were alone. But when Dennis was with us, we were obviously humanitarians, and everyone would fuss over the cute baby.

I called our social worker, asked her to set up an appointment for Benji to be retested at the Child Development Center, and said "If he's retarded—which we don't believe—if he has cerebral palsy, then let's get a definite diagnosis and get started on appropriate measures to help him."

Several days later she called me back. "I got the appointment, but not for another three months." Benji was then fifteen months old and functioning on the level of a nine-month-old.

Dennis and I started as junior high youth sponsors that week and didn't want to put Benji in the nursery yet. We bundled him up and took him with us, and the kids went wild.

"It's my turn!"

"I want to hold him!"

"Pass him to me!"

They passed him around like a football, and it was obvious that "shy, withdrawn" Benji was loving the attention. When Dennis started to give the evening devotion, I had to take Benji-the-disruption for a walk.

Two weeks after Benji's arrival my surgeon called to say, "I talked to the other specialist, and he gave me the go-ahead for your surgery. I have a cancellation for tomorrow. Can you come in this afternoon for your pre-op tests?"

I started to panic but immediately turned it over to the Lord, and He gave me a marvelous peace. Bob and Joyce

Lemon (from church) had already offered to stay with the kids and were able to make the last-minute arrangements. When the doctor examined me that afternoon, he looked rather alarmed and asked, "What have you been doing? Your pulse is way too high."

"Well, since you called I've arranged for a live-in babysitter for five children, packed lunches, planned menus, and packed."

"Enough already!" he pleaded.

My surgery went well, but I had a rough night after it. My poor roommate almost died, and every time there was a crisis the nurse would bustle in, say "Go back to sleep," give me *another* shot, and care for the elderly lady. Between the aftereffects of the anesthetic and the extra shots, it was nearly two weeks before I felt fully awake.

When I came home, another church friend, Pat Harmon, was there to spend the day with me and watch the children. There were flowers and cards from the people at church, and our meals were brought in.

Several teens came over and fixed pizza for the family. Bonny McBeen brought over homemade cookies, helped Dennis fix dinner, washed the dishes, bathed the little kids, and then had her mother pick her up.

Monday morning Joyce Lemon was back to watch the little ones and do the laundry while I slept. I had been so worried about all the little things, and I remembered the lonely feelings during Tim's and Robby's hospitalizations.

But the Lord cared so much. The surgery went well; He gave me memories of love and caring to blot out those of the pain and discomfort; He replaced my fear with peace; He saw that the house was kept clean; and He taught me that even when the unexpected happened He would care for us. He cared so very much that the kids were even supplied with homemade cookies.

After my recovery, I took Benji to our pediatrician for a checkup. Dr. Cerruti's waiting room was filled with mothers trying to entertain their children while they waited. I entered the room with my beautiful, new, black son, and we were suddenly the morning's entertainment. I tried so hard to "be cool," ignore the stares, not let them "get to me," and keep Benji quiet. "Benji Wheeler!" the nurse finally called. Still striving to be "cool" and inconspicuous, I walked right into a large metal trash container and sent it clanging to the floor—definitely not "cool" or unobserved!

Dr. Cerruti raved about "Your beautiful new son!" I described Benji's background, his physical problems, and his withdrawal. While Dr. Cerruti was prescribing a decongestant for Benji's wheezing, he told me, "When a child is in an insecure environment he will often withdraw—it's easier than coping. The best thing for Benji is to take him out often, expose him to an overdose of people, and *pass him around like a football.*"

I started laughing and had to explain, "You see, we have these junior highers, and that's exactly what they do."

Once again, God had supplied the answer before we had even defined the need.

Two months later I took Benji in for a recheck, and he had grown three inches and gained four pounds. Dr. Cerruti held the screaming Benji and said, "You know, Benji, half the world just needs some lovin', and the other half is usually afraid to give it. You're one of the lucky ones!"

On a later visit, Dr. Cerruti sounded almost poetic: "Benji, watching you grow has been like watching a little dormant bulb grow and blossom into a beautiful flower—Benji the flower child."

Dear Lord, what Dr. Cerruti is saying is so true. What special plans do You have in store for this beautiful child when he's through blossoming and growing?

That summer, C.B. Stack asked us to be camp deans again. The offer was tempting, but we knew it would be too hard to try to care for Benji and Becky and do our work. As we started to give our final no, Bill and Pat Harmon called. "Hey, you've had a busy year, and we think you need a break," they said. "You drive our two kids to camp, and we'll keep Becky and Benji for the week."

We went.

I directed Vacation Bible School later that summer, and "Little Doc" came to help. We had promised to drive her home, and she extended an invitation: "Stay for the weekend. I'd love to have you all. And I'd better get you there before you get so many kids you won't fit into my house."

It took both of our compact cars to transport the eight of us, Doc's dog, and all our miscellaneous possessions. We arrived at Doc's mountain home late that evening and spent the brief time between arrival and bedtime trying to keep Benji out of Doc's lifetime collection of knickknacks and memorabilia.

Early Saturday morning we took the children for a walk, and I carried Benji to the big field between Doc's house and the barn. Hoping to make up for the inside restrictions, I put Benji down, pointed to the open space, and told him, "Go play, Benji!"

Benji looked at all that open space, plopped down, and bawled. Poor baby, he just didn't know what to do with that much freedom. We left him alone, and after he stopped crying we saw him start playing with some tiny pebbles on the ground beside him—completely ignoring the beautiful open spaces.

Lord, how often do You have beautiful pastures for us and out of fear, like Benji, we settle for the safety of nearby pebbles?

On Sunday we attended services at the lovely church in

Greely Hill. We integrated the church and almost doubled the attendance. And we realized that along with gaining Becky and Benji, we had forfeited all rights to blend into the background and have any anonymity.

That summer we celebrated three months of having Benji, and I took him in to the Child Development Center for that long-scheduled appointment. The doctor was checking for signs and symptoms of the cerebral palsy, retardation, and emotional problems.

I immediately liked the gentle woman doctor who examined Benji. She asked scores of questions, valued my input, and was terrific with Benji.

After a very lengthy, intensive examination, we went over the list of Benji's original problems:

retarded: "There are no longer any indications that this child is retarded! I'll see that the label is officially removed!"

emotional: "You told me that Benji refused to look at himself in the mirror. That's a significant sign that we use to measure a very young child's self-image. I notice today that he's in love with his mirror image. He's very friendly, very outgoing, and on a normal sleep schedule. I see no signs of the withdrawal that was present when he was previously tested."

breathing problems: "These seem to have all cleared up after your doctor prescribed a decongestant and changed him to soymilk."

digestive problems: "There's nothing physically wrong with Benji's digestive system, and you tell me that he's tolerated the change to junior foods."

cerebral palsy: "I see a slight stiffness in his ankles, but that's all that remains of that problem."

"Doctor," I interjected, "I have two other children with cerebral palsy, and theirs hasn't just disappeared. Do you think a mistake was made in the original diagnosis?"

She read through Benji's file, shook her head, and turned to me. "No. I don't think a mistake was made about that. There were too many symptoms, too many thorough exams made by too many qualified specialists. Apparently the damaged parts of Benji's brain have effectively been taken over by the undamaged parts. All that's left is a slight stiffness in his ankles. Let him go barefoot as much as possible, and that should take care of itself."

age level: "Nine months? That's the level he was functioning on when you got him three months ago, right? After all my testing today, I would say that your eighteen-month-old son is functioning *on age level.* Nine months development in just three months! Take your son home—and enjoy!"

> Now glory be to God who by his mighty
> power at work within us is able to do
> far more than we would ever dare to ask
> or ever dream of—infinitely beyond our
> highest prayers, desires, thoughts, or
> hopes.
>
> Ephesians 3:20

We had promised our junior highers a paint party, and they were told to bring their own paint, brushes, and grubbiest clothes. "We'll supply the food," we said.

And on the big day: "There's the back fence. You can paint pictures, graffiti, anything you want. Just no nasty words." Their parents thought we were rather odd, but the kids loved it.

They painted the fence and each other, and we had a six-foot-high religious tract. While seventeen teens were busy painting, our doorbell rang.

"Hi! I'm Uncle Warren," the visitor said. "You must be Julie."

"No, but come on in. I'll take you to Mr. Wheeler."

Dennis's brother was on temporary duty in San Francisco. The brothers hadn't seen each other in eleven years. Warren knew that our oldest was about thirteen, so as he walked through the house he would introduce himself to the paint-speckled kids as "Uncle Warren."

As the bewildered man walked out on the deck, there were seventeen kids painting graffiti on the fence. Then these two black kids yelled out excitedly, "You must be *our* Uncle Warren!" Poor man thought he had wandered into Alice's tea party.

Dennis has an uncanny rapport with kids, and any success we have with them is deservedly his. Benji was smitten with Daddy and always tries to imitate him. One Saturday the two of them went shopping, and they were both dressed in blue sweatshirts and cords. My Scandinavian husband and our gorgeous dark son got scores of questioning glances as Benji proudly proclaimed to the Saturday shoppers, "I look just lika me Daddy!"

We were all gathered in the family room on one occasion, and Dennis was sitting on the floor. His little "look-alike" bounded across the room, plopped on Daddy's lap, and announced, "Here I is, ready or not! Love me!"

Someone once tried, unsuccessfully, to tease Benji about his daddy. "Do you *think* your daddy loves you?"

"Nope!" Benji adamantly answered.

"Aw, come on, Benji. Don't you really *think* your daddy loves you?"

With another vigorous shake of his head, Benji again answered, "Nope! I *know him love me!*"

When I first heard that Benji would be arriving with only one outfit, I had prayed, *Lord, do I have a prayer request for You.* The Lord has honored that prayer, continually and abundantly.

All the other children had blue windbreakers. One fall afternoon, as I was getting the children ready to go to the park, I said, *Lord, we need to get a blue windbreaker for Benji.*

The next morning Sandy Bras brought over a big parcel of clothes for Benji, and guess what was right on top. One blue windbreaker? No. Four!

Another morning, Benji was getting dressed, and I noticed the condition of his undershirts. *Lord, guess we need to get him some T-shirts.* The next week we received five.

There have been several frightening times with Benji: a serious hip infection that prevented him from walking; an unexplained fever that went over 105 degrees and wouldn't come down; and a mysterious anemia that had the doctors checking for the dread sickle cell trait.

In such times my mother's heart will start to tremble and panic, fear will start to take over, and then I'll hear that patient, loving voice say, *If I care enough to provide blue windbreakers and white T-shirts, can't you trust Me with this?*

It's so easy with a large family to treat the children as a big group: girls, boys, oldest, youngest. We've tried to recognize individuality by giving each person his day to say the blessing at dinner. Benji learned about "Timmyday" and "Robbyday" long before he knew Monday and Tuesday.

At breakfast and lunch, Benji will often beg, *"Please,* let me say grace, Mommy." When I give permission, his chubby little face glows. Then he bows his head, scrunches his eyes shut, and prays, "Dear God, mumble, mumble, amen." Then he turns to me and says, "Oh, thank you for letting me pray."

Dear Lord, when I tell Benji he can pray, he acts as if I've given him one of the world's treasures—and I have. We think we have more comprehension than little Benji, our pronunciation is clearer, we know more theology. But Benji has the joy. Oh, Lord, give us Benji's joy in praying.

There were a few minor conflicts when Benji first arrived. He thought that anyone on the floor was there to play with him. So every time he would see Becky sitting on the floor, he would give her a push and she would fall right over. He thought it was a delightful game. Becky didn't.

We finally convinced Becky of her family security, but she was concerned about the newcomer. "How long does he get to stay?" she asked more than once. When Benji started to dress himself and was getting more independent, Becky suddenly became very helpful. "Come here, Benji. Let me do that for you."

Becky was worried that the baby was soon going to pass her up, and we had to achieve the delicate balance between soothing her fragile ego and encouraging Benji's independence.

"Mommy! Look at this! I can't even touch my toes." Julie was trying to do her exercises and was getting increasingly upset at her inability to touch those elusive toes.

Benji watched quietly while Julie struggled and grew more upset. Then a look of compassion swept over his face and he told her, "Don't cry, Julie. I'll touch dem for you!"

To Julie's amazement, Benji walked over and very seriously got down on his knees and touched her toes.

"OK, Julie?" asked the littlest Samaritan.

Benji has an amazing ability to make friends, and one of his favorites is "Marsha the Missionary." Marsha Speilman has a children's ministry in Mexico, and we met her the first year that we worked at camp with C.B. Stack. Marsha comes to the States to speak at missionary conferences, and we're usually fortunate enough to get a brief visit each year.

Marsha has an unusual rapport with little ones, especially Benji. Whenever Marsha mentions a Spanish phrase, Benji will copy her with nearly perfect inflection.

After one of her visits, we all took Marsha to the airport

and stayed to watch the plane leave. For the next year Benji would yell at every airplane, "There goes my Marsha." On her next visit Benji was a little older—but no less in love. "Marsha, I wuv you. I go to Me-hi-co wif you?"

"Benji, you can't go with me. Think how much your mommy and daddy would miss you."

"Don't care 'bout them"—the ingrate—"Wanta go wif you."

Last fall when Marsha arrived, we wondered how the older Benji would react. Marsha brought her newly adopted son with her, and we all anxiously awaited Benji's reaction to this new arrival. Benji was terrific with Nathan: he gave him lots of attention, held his bottle, and asked to hold him. We were all surprised at the seeming lack of jealousy.

Shortly before they left, Benji sat beside Marsha while she was feeding Nathan. "You know, Marsha, he's a nice baby," my little cherub said.

"Thank you, Benji. I think so, too."

"You still love me, Marsha?"

"I sure do, Ben."

"Marsha, you know when you and me go to Me-hi-co on the airplane, there ain't gonna be no room for that baby. Maybe we can leave him with my mother."

The year 1976 was packed for our family: Becky's surgery, our building program, and Dennis started a new job.

Shortly before Becky's operation, we moved Benji into the boys' room. The three of them managed to turn the room into Disaster City, and Benji was constantly getting in trouble for messing up the boys' possessions. We definitely needed another bedroom, but the city abounds in complicated building codes, and several neighbors had moved because they couldn't get the necessary permits.

A local contractor gave us a bid, but the city refused to

issue the required permit. We prayed for the Lord's will while the ever hopeful contractor camped out at city hall. We knew the Lord would provide the elusive permit and the required finances if the addition was His will.

After a month's stalemate the jubilant contractor called with the permits, and construction began. We would gain two more bedrooms, another bathroom, a large storage closet, and a small office for me.

As the building progressed, there were myriads of extras that weren't covered by the bank loan but required cash: carpets, linoleum, gallons of paint, furniture, window coverings, and so on. Once again we were allowed to see the Lord's abundance.

Our original prayer was, *Lord, we know You can answer these prayers, but we really don't see how.* At the same time I had been praying for Becky's surgery and Dennis's job situation.

Dennis received a call at about that time from a previous employer who wanted to create a position for Dennis. At first I had asked, *Lord, why is everything happening at once?* But we soon saw His perfect plan unfolding as money came in from so many unconnected sources that we had to recognize God as the *ultimate source:*

•Dennis got a company car, and we sold our second car five minutes after we put up the "For Sale" sign.

•Dennis received severance and vacation pay when he changed jobs.

•Because of the refinancing, we went two months without a house payment.

•I went to close out a savings account, and they had made an error in our favor.

> For if you give, you will get!
> Your gift will return to you in full
> and overflowing measure, pressed down,

shaken together to make room for more,
and running over.

Luke 6:38

We were able to witness in many different ways during the
construction period. We even saw the workers standing on
the roof "reading" our fence during their coffee breaks.

I had written Luke 6:38 on the kitchen bulletin board, and
one worker commented, "Gee, lady, I've read lots of the Bible, but I never saw a verse like that before."

And there was Benji, the miniature expert on race relationships. There was an older man who was a real taskmaster with
the work crew. I would often hear him screaming, so I tried
extra hard to keep the ever curious Benji out of his way.

One morning I lost Benji. I called and called before he
finally answered. "Where have you been?" I demanded.

"Coffee break, Mommy. Coffee break."

Same time the next morning—no Benji. When I started to
investigate, I heard the "bear's" voice and thought, *Oh, no!
Benji's had it now.*

There sat Benji with the bear (who turned out to be a pan-
da in disguise). "Hi, Mrs. Wheeler. I hope you don't mind,
but every morning this little guy joins me for my coffee
break." There sat Benji, grinning from ear to ear and drink-
ing his share of the coffee from the red Thermos cup.

Finally! Construction was finished. The house was clean
again, and we had six bedrooms and three baths. Benji had
his own room, Tim and Robby were sharing a room, and
there was one empty bedroom downstairs. We painted the
room blue and decorated it with Holly Hobby dolls. Then we
told our social worker, "We'd like another little girl, and this
time we don't care about the age, race, or handicap." As a
joke I added, "After the very vocal Becky, I wouldn't mind a
deaf-mute."

That summer Dennis's mother came out from

Massachusetts for a visit. We had wondered how she would respond to her newest grandchildren. We shouldn't have worried; she loves them all.

Becky and Benji acted as though "Grammy" was someone they had personally given us. They loved hearing stories about "When your daddy was little," being held on Grammy's lap, and eating her Swedish cookies.

During that winter of 1976, Dennis got sick, really sick, for the first time in our married life. He had viral pneumonia, acute bronchitis, pleurisy, and a collapsed lung. He was off work for over two months, and since he had only been with the company since May, we were concerned about his job and our finances. But the people in the company were terrific. They reassured Dennis about his job, called often, and kept sending the paychecks.

Dennis and I have a very supportive, interdependent relationship, and that was the first time I hadn't been able to depend on him. I had to be the strong one, and I didn't like it! I had all the responsibilities for the kids, the car, and the budget. I was overwhelmed by the multitude of it all and my concern for Dennis.

Lord, I'm so very tired. Did You ever feel this way? And I saw Jesus hanging on the cross with not just all of *my* burdens and sins, but those of the whole world.

Suddenly my load was made lighter by just knowing that my Heavenly Comforter understood.

> I am your God. I will strengthen you;
> I will help you; I will uphold you with
> my victorious right hand.
>
> Isaiah 41:10

"Hey, Mom! Come and watch Benji!"

I ran out front to find that Timmy had used his tool kit and taken the training wheels off Benji's bike. Robby was running alongside Benji, who was proudly riding his two-wheeler. Dennis and I stood unashamedly teary-eyed, watching Benji do what so many experts said he would never do; watching Timmy's and Robby's pride in Benji's accomplishment; watching Benji do what most people consider commonplace, but what for us was all an impossible dream come true.

Every time Benji has said a new word or taken another step of progress, we've all felt that we have just witnessed a miracle. I've even started feeling sorry for people who take a child's progress for granted and miss out on the miraculous.

We have learned so many precious lessons about speech, sturdy legs, and bright minds. And what treasures they all are. Our family has gained a unique sense of accomplishment with Benji. We supplied the love and watched God supply the miracles.

After dinner one day I asked, "Does anyone have something special to praise the Lord for?"

Benji waved his little arm.

"OK, Benji. What do you want to praise the Lord for?"

Benji-the-humble answered for us all, *"Me!"*

We had applied to adopt another child, but we first had to go to court and make Becky's and Benji's adoptions final. There had been an incredible amount of legal snags and delays. On July 19, 1977, we finally went to court and saw Becky and Benji become our "legally and forever" children.

The kids were all dressed in their best clothes as we were ushered into the judge's chambers. The judge talked to us all, asked a few questions, signed the necessary papers, and passed out jelly beans.

By the time we had all shaken hands, Becky and Benji were both covered with jelly bean goo. But they were ours. Dennis took us all out for a celebration lunch, and the waitresses gave the children the royal treatment.

Any apprehensions that we had about raising a black child

were dispelled the next Sunday. "Hello, welcome to our church," I greeted the newcomer. As we walked toward our car, Benji saw me talking to this lovely—and very black—lady and yelled, "Hey Mommy! Is that your mommy?" Benji doesn't realize he's any different from us. He just thinks we all look like him.

Whenever we mention Becky's and Benji's color, we always make positive comments, and it's paying off. We got new placemats (each a different color) and I told the kids, "Pick your color." Benji quickly picked the brown one, flashed that beautiful smile, and said, "Pretty brown boys should have pretty brown placemats!"

A friend once asked Becky, "Are there any other Beckys at your church?"

"Yes," she replied, "there's one."

"Is she as pretty as you?"

"No, she's white."

We talk honestly and openly about Benji's and Becky's adoption, but Benji doesn't really believe us. "You know, Benji, you're black and I'm white."

"Uh-uh!" was his emphatic reply.

"Look at my arm next to yours."

"Uh-uh!"

"Well, how about I'm pink and you're brown?"

"Uh-uh!"

"I give up! Benji, what are we?"

Benji looked at me with those beautiful big eyes, smiled that gorgeous, heart-stopping smile, and ignored all the color lines, all the birth lines.

"You're my mommy, and I your Benji."

8
Melissa

"BONNIE, THIS IS Sandy Cardoza. May Ron and I come over tonight? We need to talk to you."

"Dennis, I wonder what the Cardozas want to talk about? We're not usually so formal with each other."

That Sunday evening, in October 1976, after the cake was served and the coffee was poured, Sandy started explaining. "We've met this little girl that we're hoping to get as a foster child. She's eight years old, deaf, blind, and retarded. We wanted to talk to you because of your experience with Becky and Benji."

"Sandy, that sounds like too much to me," I replied. "I couldn't handle all of that. Give it a lot of prayer, and make sure you know what you're getting into. We'll be praying for you."

"I don't know how to explain her," said Sandy, "but there's just something about Melissa. Here's a picture."

Dennis and I reached out for the photo. It showed hacked off, dark, tangled hair; two hearing aids with wires running down her neck; glasses; and a grossly underweight body. I thought to myself, *Sandy sure can't love Melissa for her looks.* But I replied to Sandy, "She's so tiny."

That night I entered Melissa's name in my prayer journal, and for the next few months I prayed for both the little girl we were hoping for *and* this child that Ron and Sandy cared so much about. Little did we realize how God would answer that prayer.

Sandy and Ron went through most of the licensing process, finally getting to the time when a social worker came to their house. The interview went well until the worker passed through the family room and saw the backyard.

"You didn't tell me about the swimming pool!" she accused.

"Nobody ever asked," replied the surprised Sandy.

"It would never do to place a child like Melissa in a home with a pool. She couldn't see the pool, she couldn't hear you yell a warning, and she wouldn't understand if you told her to stay away. We made an exception one time, with fatal results. I'm sorry, but it's out of the question!"

In May our social worker called us. "Bonnie, remember you once said that you'd like a deaf-mute?" she asked. "Were you serious? I have some information here on an eight-year-old girl who's deaf. Would you and Dennis be interested?"

Without hesitating I replied, "Please get the information."

I called Sandy and told her, "What a funny coincidence. I wonder how many eight-year-old deaf girls there are in the area?"

A few weeks later our worker called with more information, and I asked, "Is the child's name, by any chance, Melissa?"

There was a stunned silence on the other end, then, "Good grief! How did you know that?"

This was the same child Ron and Sandy wanted. The same child that I'd tried to talk Sandy out of. The same child I had been praying for all those months. When our worker checked with Melissa's social worker she was informed, "I've recently received that name. The Wheelers were referred to us by AASK [Aid to Adoption of Special Kids]."

I asked Dennis, "Do meaningless coincidences happen to Christians? Why would this child keep coming up if God doesn't have a special purpose?"

We had several long talks with Ron and Sandy. "Our friendship is very special," we said. "Can you handle it if we would get Melissa?"

They both assured us, "Melissa needs a home. If we can't have her, it would be great if you guys could."

I was desperately praying, *Dear God, are You planning what I think You're planning? I really don't believe I can handle this.*

Dennis confided, "I know it's too early and we haven't seen her yet, but I have a feeling that she's going to be number six." Now I really started praying in earnest and trying to understand God's plan.

Masterplan

"Oh, God, what is Your purpose?
Oh, Lord, what is Your plan?
This is not what I'd have chosen,
Help me to understand."
This answer came so quickly,
From Isaiah's words of old:
"My thoughts are not your thoughts
My ways are not your ways.
Just as the heavens are higher
Than the earth,
So my ways are higher than yours,
And my thoughts than yours."
"Oh, God, what is Your purpose?
Oh, Lord, what is Your plan?
This is not what I'd have chosen,
Help me to understand."
"This will make the Lord's name

Very great
And be an everlasting sign
Of God's power and love."
"Oh, God, what is Your purpose?
Oh, Lord, what is Your plan?
This is what You have chosen,
Help me obey Your command."

In June we received a fact sheet on Melissa: "deaf-blind,
rubella syndrome, congenital heart defect, functionally
retarded." Dennis and I read the information; his face mir-
rored my fear. These were all new words, new problems.
"Oh, Dennis," I said. "Nothing has prepared us for this!"

Melissa's social worker gave us the name of Melissa's
teacher, and I gave her a call. When I first heard about
Melissa I immediately reread the story of Helen Keller, and
I'll always think of Norma Johnson as Melissa's Anne
Sullivan.

Norma raved about Melissa's potential and told us, "She
has peripheral vision in her left eye—that means she can see
out of the side of that eye. The other eye is covered with an
opacity (like a cataract) and has no vision at all. Melissa can
hear when you clap your hands or call her name. She has a
lovely laugh but will probably never talk."

"What does 'functionally retarded' mean, and how does it
differ from 'mentally retarded?' " I asked.

"It means she's functioning below her age level due to the
communications problems. A mentally retarded child will
eventually level off. Melissa has unlimited potential, and
with deaf-blind children like her the problem is not the
severity of each separate handicap but the overwhelming
communication problem resulting from any combination of
visual and hearing impairments. If there's anything I can do
to help, I will."

I read over the fact sheet again and tried to balance it with the superoptimistic conversation I'd just had. The cold facts still scared us, but that night Dennis and I talked things over. More than once we came back to the thought, *What if our whole future—our only real chance—depended on what someone had written on one piece of paper?*

Dennis and I gave the situation much prayer, and then we asked our social workers to set up a meeting with Melissa's worker. We were again cautioned, "This child is very involved. Be careful and make sure you aren't taking on too much."

Melissa's worker looked around our living room with its dozens of lush plants and remarked, "Well, if you're as good with kids as you are with plants, you've got my vote." I spent the next month caring for those plants with a new intensity. *Lord,* I prayed, *please don't let these plants die now.*

Our worker also warned, "You can't do anything about this child until after your court date to finalize Becky's and Benji's adoptions. It won't hurt anything to see Melissa, but plan on taking it slow and easy. We have to do a whole new home study, and that will take at least six months."

We made an appointment to go to Melissa's summer school and see her on July 11, 1977. I arrived at the school before the others, and as I sat and waited I was almost overwhelmed with feelings of panic. Around the corner came a man walking with a child. I could make out glasses and the double wires from two hearing aids, but I couldn't see the child's face. The child's arms were flailing the air, and the child could barely walk.

Dear God, if that's Melissa, I know I can't handle her. Then I thought, *I know what. I'll leave right now and just let everyone think I got lost and couldn't find the school.*

As the man and child got closer to my car, I saw that it wasn't Melissa. Just as I sighed with relief, Dennis and the social workers arrived and I lost my chance to escape.

I had prayed that if this was *the* child that the Lord wanted for us, He would give us that special feeling of recognition we'd had with Becky and Benji. I especially prayed, *Lord, work through Dennis and convince him if Melissa's the one.*

That first visit at Melissa's school went well, and that in itself was a miracle. There were three social workers observing the whole scene; the summer school teacher and his aide were trying to teach; Norma Johnson was there to interpret in sign language for us; and Dennis and I were there to check out Melissa.

Melissa was eating a snack when we first arrived, and we had a good chance to observe her. Her hair was a short, matted mess. Her summer top was winter's top with the sleeves chopped off. The lenses of her glasses were badly scratched, and the body (hearing) aids she was wearing made two square lumps under her shirt.

Melissa ate very neatly, very precisely (she looked like a little old lady at a tea party!), and when she finished she wiped off her placemat, put it away, washed and dried her hands, then came to see Norma.

"These are my friends," Norma signed as Melissa came over to investigate the invaders in her classroom. Melissa has a real "thing" about hands, and she immediately checked us all out. After she had examined the social workers, she decided to concentrate on Dennis and me. Then I was discarded. Like Becky and Benji before, she sensed something special about Dennis.

If I would ask for a hug, Melissa would come to me. She would *run* to Dennis and throw her skinny little arms around him. She would let me hold her hand, but she would *take* Dennis's. We went out to the playground, and she declared Dennis her own personal property. He had to push the swing; he had to watch her slide. Melissa fell for Dennis's warmth, his love, and the bright red light on his digital watch.

Watching Dennis get acquainted with his new daughter—I was finally giving in to the inevitable—I was reminded of the Gaither song line, "He looked beyond my faults and saw my needs."

I wanted to hug her, fix that matted hair, and put her in some pretty clothes. Dennis simply said, "She needs us."

After our visit, Dennis and I went out for lunch to sort through our first impressions. As we left the restaurant to get in our separate cars, Dennis yelled across the parking lot, "I think we're going to have another child. Congratulations!"

On July 19, we went to court to make final Becky's and Benji's adoptions. I've never been called a patient person, and everyone had told us we couldn't do anything about Melissa until after the court date. On July 20, I was back at Melissa's school and went shopping with her class. I was surprised at how well we could communicate even though I knew no sign language and she couldn't speak. Because Melissa is so very nearsighted, whenever she would see something at the store that caught her interest, she would practically lay her eye on it. The term "eyeballing the merchandise" took on a whole new meaning.

When we were considering the adoptions of Becky and Benji, it seemed that everyone we knew had the same message: "You have a lot to handle right now. Are you sure you can handle another child?" When we got Becky and Benji, we both felt confident that with God's help we could handle another child. We believed that all we had experienced with our first three children had prepared us to cope with Becky and Benji.

Now, faced with Melissa, Dennis and I were both doing a lot of soul searching. "Can we really handle this child? Have we met our limit?" But every time we would express those fears and concerns to anyone else, we were optimistically reassured, "Hey, relax! Look at Becky and Benji."

Despite those reassurances, Dennis and I remained scared and concerned about our capabilities to deal with the multiplicity of Melissa's problems, and a refrain kept playing leapfrog through our minds, *Can we cope? There is hope. Can we cope? There is hope.* We saw Melissa a few more times and decided it was essential that she become part of a family as soon as possible.

Melissa's foster home was a mini-institution with all deaf-blind children. The home was clean and the kids were well cared for. But the three ladies working eight-hour shifts just couldn't make it a home. With both Melissa's classroom and home inhabited exclusively by deaf-blind children, she was prepared only to live in a deaf-blind world.

Out of necessity, the home operated for the lowest level child. Many rubella children have chewing problems, so everyone's food was put through a blender. Many rubella kids are incontinent, so the bathroom doors were locked and all the children were put in night diapers. Many deaf-blind children will never be independent, so everything was done for the children. There were no chores, no responsibilities, no discipline, no stimulation, and no interaction.

Deaf-blind children are usually in their private little world and don't play with each other, so Melissa had no interaction with other children. She seemed to learn best by imitation, but there was little in her present world to imitate. We were afraid that another six months in that sterile, deaf-blind world would be too much for Melissa and could be the difference between a hopeless and a hope-filled future.

Dennis was on vacation the first two weeks in August, and we had made plans to travel to Arizona to visit friends. The week before we were to leave, we were warned by at least five different people not to go there in August—"The heat will be too much!" Since our children all act terminally ill when

the temperature goes over 85 degrees, we decided to stay
home and take day trips.

The first morning of Dennis's vacation, we talked more
about Melissa and decided to call our worker and see what
could be done to speed things up. Dennis told me, "You call
and I'll pray."

Early Monday morning, Dennis sat on one side of the bed
and prayed, and I called our social worker. "Dennis and I
have been doing a lot of talking and praying," I said, "and
we're very concerned about Melissa's staying in that environment for another six months. Is there any way she can be
placed in our home sooner?"

Our poor worker was silent for a moment, then answered,
"I don't know if there's anything we can do to speed up the
process, but I'll check with my supervisor and see."

She was hardly encouraging and I wrote in my prayer journal, *"Lord, if You really want us to have this child, let her
join our family by the end of this month."*

Tuesday morning we planned to go to Great America (a
nearby amusement park), and I wanted to call the social
worker before we left. "No!" Dennis told me, "don't push
it."

We packed our sweaters, loaded up the five kids, and I ran
back for my sunglasses. As I started back out the front door,
the phone rang. "Hello!" said the voice on the other end of
the line. "This is your social worker. I talked to Melissa's
worker, and we're turning the case over to their department.
You should hear from them tomorrow."

Early Wednesday morning, Melissa's worker called and
said, "We've all talked it over and feel that it's essential for
Melissa to be part of a family just as soon as possible. I'm going to court Friday, and we'll get an order from the judge
placing Melissa in your home immediately. I'll bring her out
for a couple of visits next week, and she can move in on

Thursday." (Exactly two weeks *before* the "deadline" I had asked of the Lord! He loved and cared about us so very much that He not only answered that specific prayer but was also delivering the answer early.)

When Melissa came for her first visit to our house, I was apprehensive about how the children would react. Melissa was in her own little world and had several "blindisms" that would seem strange to them.

Timmy gave up a birthday party: "I'd rather see her for the day"; Robby stayed in the backyard: "So I can play with my new sister"; Becky let Melissa explore her room and examine all her prized toys: "Because poor Melissa doesn't have any"; Benji wasn't the least jealous: "Does she get to stay?"; and Melissa promptly claimed Julie as her exclusive property.

When Melissa came to our house for that first visit, we let her tour the house at her own pace. She checked out the upstairs rooms; then the family room, living room, kitchen, and our room got cursory glances. She lingered a little in Becky's and Benji's room, saw the bathroom, used it, and washed and dried her hands.

Next on her agenda was the remaining downstairs room—the empty blue room that we had lovingly and expectantly decorated with blue gingham spread, curtains, and Holly Hobby dolls.

Melissa walked into the room; seemed to sense something special; and checked out every square inch, every doll, every toy. Then she went over to the blue-covered bed and stretched out. She'd staked her claim.

"Why has she taken to this room?" we asked each other. "No one's told her this will be her room, and she doesn't have enough language to understand if we did tell her."

Norma Johnson explained, "In the classroom, all the kids' possessions are color-coded: their toothbrush, glass, placemat, cupboard, chair. And Melissa's color code is *blue*."

When we first decided on the color scheme for that empty room, God already had Melissa's color in mind. She saw that room and knew it was hers. God used a color to communicate our welcome to a child who never could have understood our words.

We learned that day that when you really step out in faith and trust God in spite of your fears, He directs the smallest details of your life, chooses just the right color, and gives you color-coded miracles.

Melissa spent the night with us, and we took her shopping for a new outfit. That night I shampooed her hair and watched her take a bath. In the familiar confines of the bathtub, she doesn't have to worry about her lack of vision or hearing. She's like a baby seal: laughing, splashing, floating on her back. We saw the scars from her open-heart surgery, and one of the kids remarked, "She looks like a patchwork quilt."

The next morning we took Melissa back to her foster home to meet with the social worker, pack her things, and say good-bye to the people who had cared for her for almost five years. Melissa walked in, saw the lady, was hugged, and then threw the biggest temper tantrum we had ever seen.

The poor lady did everything she could think of to make Melissa stop. Nothing worked. Melissa lay on the floor for twenty minutes, screaming, twisting, and kicking everything in reach.

Good grief! If I'd seen this before, I might not have said yes.

Melissa's social worker warned us, "This was on that fact sheet. This show is repeated two or three times each day."

There were several theories that day. "She senses what's going on and is upset by all the things she can't understand," maintained one social worker. Another theory was, "She's afraid that returning means she's not going to stay with you." Needless to say, we liked that last theory best.

When it was time to leave, Dennis picked the still-screaming Melissa up off the floor, held her tight, and firmly told her, "You stop that, we're going home now." She immediately stopped the tantrum, clung to Dennis, and had him carry her to the car.

While I was praying for the advent of this sixth child, I had claimed a verse for her as I had for the others. Melissa's verse was about the "ninety and nine." When she walked into our house that afternoon, I was reminded of that verse and how very much God cared for that one little lost lamb.

Melissa reminds me of the little lambs that the Good Shepherd cared for: lovable, helpless, meek, not communicative, needing the constant watch of the Shepherd. But oh, how the Shepherd loves those little lambs.

Dennis was home that first weekend and was a great help with Melissa's initial adjustment. We had thought that Julie's orthopedic problems had prepared us to cope with Becky. Nothing prepared us for Melissa.

In the group home that Melissa lived in, all the closet doors and dresser drawers were locked shut. Rooms that were off limits were kept locked, and all the rooms were stripped down to the bare essentials.

For the first month, Melissa explored every square inch of our house. We have about two thousand square feet of living space, and although I'm no mathematician, that adds up to a lot of square inches for a curious little girl to investigate. There wasn't a drawer, closet, or box that she didn't inspect. We had no idea how much we could trust Melissa, and we were constantly on watch. She was also constantly taking off her shoes and socks and refusing to play with her toys.

I spent those first days trying to keep track of her, making her put those shoes and socks back on, and trying to interest her in her new toys.

At night Melissa would play and giggle until midnight,

sleep for two or three hours, and declare the rest of the night "play time." She would get into her closet and try on all the new shoes and socks—now she wants them on!—laugh, giggle, and have a grand time with her new toys—now she wants to play!

I have always needed eight hours sleep, and getting my sleep abruptly cut back to two or three hours was almost too much for me. Many nights I would walk the dark halls, crying, *Lord, I'm so very tired. I can't manage this. I can't make it through tonight, much less tomorrow.*

His loving, patient answer was always the same. *I know you can't my child, but I can. Depend on My strength, not your own.*

Then He would remind me of Isaiah 41:9-10:

> I have chosen you and will not
> throw you away.
> Fear not, for I am with you.
> Do not be dismayed. I am your
> God. I will strengthen you; I
> will help you; I will uphold you
> with my victorious right hand.

And I'd make it through another night.

Because of the central nervous system damage, rubella kids (as a group) require very little sleep. And because of the hearing and vision impairments, it's hard for them to differentiate between night and day and get on a normal cycle.

Most nights I would sit in the chair beside Melissa's bed, trying to establish the habit, "This is nighttime, and you have to stay in bed and be quiet whether you sleep or not."

One night, in sleepy desperation, I sat a big doll in the chair by Melissa's bed and tiptoed out of the room, hoping my ruse might get me a few hours of sleep. (She only fell for my ruse one time.)

Melissa finally decided that if she could keep me from

knowing she was up, I would leave her alone. *Slam! Bang!* I jumped out of bed, thinking that the house was exploding. It was Melissa, slamming the doors so I wouldn't know she was up. She didn't realize that just because she couldn't hear the doors slam didn't mean that I couldn't either.

In the group home, all the children were put into diapers and the bathroom door was locked at night. I told Melissa's social worker and Norma, "Melissa has such good control during the day; she should be able to make it through the night. I don't care what her problems are, but as long as she's not incontinent, I'm not buying diapers for a nine-year-old."

"Give it a try!" they both urged.

That first night, Melissa lifted her legs for me to diaper her. "No way!" I said as I handed her thick panties. "Put your legs down and put these on yourself!"

She screamed and hollered because I'd broken her routine, but she eventually put them on. And the bedding was soaked the next morning. And the next. And the next.

I soon discovered that it took Melissa about three or four hours to get to sleep. As soon as she wet she would wake up, and then she would stay awake. Since I wasn't getting much sleep anyway, I decided to try to train her. When Melissa woke up at 3 A.M., I would get her up and send her to the bathroom. Then I'd have her put on dry clothes and put her back to bed. After about two months of this effort, Melissa was able to throw away the rubber pants and stay dry through most nights.

When we celebrated Melissa's birthday, she didn't seem aware of what was going on. She liked playing with the wrappers and ribbons and went after everyone's hands.

We've tried to rationalize and understand Melissa's love of hands, but not always successfully. Whenever Melissa sees new people, she automatically checks their hands. She looks for callouses, fingernail polish, and rings. Part of her obsession with hands seems to be a means of communication. Through signing, hands are her only means of communication; and it's self-stimulation, a habit of the blind.

Shortly after Melissa moved into our home, we started seeing something we had hoped for become reality. We had all believed that it was essential for Melissa to have more positive peer modeling since she learns best by imitation (and had had so little to imitate).

One afternoon I sat her down at the table and gave her color crayons and a coloring book. She seemed to enjoy it but either scribbled or drew hands. The next afternoon, Becky and Benji sat at the table and colored with Melissa. Melissa watched them and colored almost as well as they did—remarkable with her limited vision. Then the same thing started happening at Sunday school. She would watch the other children for cues and would color when they did, wait for grace to be said, eat her snack, and throw away her trash.

The whole process of saying grace must be very confusing for Melissa with her limited communication skills. From her viewpoint, we have this good food in front of us, and instead of eating right away we fold our hands, close our eyes, and say words she neither hears nor comprehends.

But she's catching on. She's not sure what this strange custom is, but she's learning to use it. One evening she wanted more food, and instead of signing the word *more* she folded her hands and bowed her head. Another evening, Julie had her hands in her lap during grace, and Melissa waited with her hands folded and her head bowed. Melissa looked over (she thinks it's totally unnecessary to close her eyes), saw Julie with her hands in her lap, and started hitting Julie with her folded hands. Julie got the message.

The sign for "on" is made by *lightly* laying the palm of your right hand on top of the back of your left hand. Melissa still delighted in taking off her shoes and socks, and one day she actually removed them twenty-five times, completely wrecking the elastic in the new socks.

That evening, Dennis noticed that the top of my left hand was horribly bruised. "What happened to you?" he naturally asked.

"Well, Melissa kept taking off her shoes and socks, and every time I told her to put them back on, I'd get a little angrier and sign 'on' even harder."

Dennis and I were concerned that we seemed to be constantly saying no to Melissa. At the group home she had no discipline, and there had been little to get into. Here there was plenty to get into, and she decided to find out what the house rules were, then test them all.

Once, after a particularly trying day, I signed "no" and Melissa looked at me, stomped her feet, and signed a long string of "No! No! No!"—backtalk in sign language and the first time I was ever encouraged by a sassy child.

Now if she gets upset with me, she either turns her back to me so she can't see my signs or turns off her hearing aid. We also have a goodly number of arguments. She will sign for a cookie before dinner, and I'll sign "no." Melissa will then sign "yes" and we'll go back and forth. When she gets tired of this, Melissa will take my hands and form the signs for "cookie" and "yes," then run over to the cookie jar.

To balance out all the no's we had added to Melissa's life, we used lots and lots of hugs, kisses, and touching with her. "How can we teach the meaning of love to a child who's never had a family and doesn't know the meaning of love?" we asked each other. We hoped to communicate to Melissa through actions what we couldn't with words. She didn't kiss, and although she would let herself be hugged, she either didn't hug back or she would put her arms around our necks and play with her hands while we hugged her. In the group home, all the chairs were small wooden ones, and I don't think she had even had the experience of sitting on laps, being rocked, and held. And there had been no men in her life.

Melissa was starved for all that touching, stroking, and loving. The first night that she was sick with a high fever, I was trying to calm her down while the medicine worked. Not knowing what else to do, I took her to the old rocking chair to see if that would soothe her. Like magic, she took her skinny little fevered body, curled up in a fetal position, and seemed to melt into me as we rocked. I always sang to the children when I rocked them, and I did that with Melissa. I started to cry as it occurred to me, *All the songs that the other children learned, she'll never even hear.*

That night I started a routine that we follow when I rock her. I talk to Melissa about Jesus, about how much we love her, about the many prayers that God answered to bring her to us—all the things I want to tell her that she neither hears nor understands. But, nonetheless, I have to tell her.

When she curls up in that fetal position, it seems that we're backtracking and going through the stages she missed. Melissa especially enjoys getting to sit on Daddy's lap.

When we asked each other how to teach the meaning of love to a child like Melissa, we really had no idea how to, or if we could. We decided to sign "I love you" every time we held, hugged, or kissed her, and prayed that it would work. We continued for months with no tangible results.

Then one golden day, Melissa came over to me and spontaneously signed, "I love you." Trumpets blared, angels sang, fireworks went off, and I felt that God had just handed me one of His choicest gifts. "I love you!"

Melissa not only learned the sign, but it's become one of her favorites. She bit the fingers off one of her dolls so that it's perpetually signing "I love you."

Melissa loves to get Julie to spin her around. Long past

when Julie's too dizzy, Melissa will sign, "One more, please." Julie's reward is hearing Melissa's infrequent but delightful giggle.

Melissa and Robby don't seem to realize that she's taller than he. One day Robby went to get her off the bus, and they both thought it would be fun for her to jump off into his arms. She did and he caught her, but they both fell to the ground, Melissa and her "big" brother.

Timmy is still slightly hyperactive and at that tough "macho" stage that teenage boys all go through. But tiny Melissa has him wrapped around her finger.

Melissa loves to play in Becky's room—not to play with Becky, just Becky's toys. When Melissa first came, Becky was grabbing hold of whatever was handy every time she started to fall. This would startle Melissa, and she would push Becky away. *Crash!* Melissa has learned—so has Becky—and is very cautious of her now.

Melissa likes and responds to the children in direct proportion to their ages. That puts Benji last, and deservedly so, for Benji decided to be Melissa's personal tormentor. He picked up some basic signs and makes the most of them. "Here's this kid much taller than me, and I can tell her 'no,'" says Benji. And he does with regularity. For months, every time Benji was around Melissa, he would look at her and sign "no!" Melissa couldn't figure out what she had done wrong, and she would get very upset. We couldn't explain Benji's pesty age to Melissa, and Benji was on a power trip.

The kids were playing in Becky's room one day, and Benji-the-pest bent over. Melissa cocked her head so she had a good view of Benji's backside. She started swinging her foot and seemed to be measuring the distance. It seemed like a good idea, so she swung back her foot and flattened him. Benji's been much more respectful ever since.

In October, Melissa's class wore Halloween costumes and

went trick or treating to the other classes. That night Dennis and I took the kids to our school carnival. We all went outside, and Melissa panicked. She screamed, ran, and literally threw herself into Dennis's arms and sobbed.

We stayed at the carnival for a while, but Dennis had to bring the still-sobbing Melissa back home. We talked to Norma Johnson to discover what had scared Melissa so badly. She had seen the costumes, and the trick or treating wasn't new. What was so different about Halloween *night?*

"Norma, has she ever been out in the dark?" I asked.

"I doubt it. The kids in the group home kept regular, early hours."

The whole time that Melissa had been with us, it had been light until almost 9 P.M., and when we go out with six children, we come home before dark. The house after dark holds no fears for Melissa, but with her limited vision, the vastness of a dark outside world is just overwhelming.

The next night we went to visit Sandy Cardoza. Melissa has been there often—in the daytime. Melissa screamed all the way over and was so scared that she trembled. I had to drag her from the van to Sandy's front door, and once we were there she curled up on my lap and sobbed.

It took over two months to get Melissa to accept going outside after dark. Melissa has no depth perception, and when she sees a curb or a crack in the sidewalk, she doesn't know if it's a six-inch step or six feet. Knowing that the dark is full of unseen terrors was just too much for Melissa. Experience is important for every child, and doubly so for Melissa.

Every morning for almost two years, Melissa has gone down our driveway to get on her school bus. At first she paused on the front step, hesitated at the curb. After all those mornings she can now *run* to the bus.

The Christmas holidays took on a special joy that year as we all saw and celebrated Christmas through Melissa's eyes. Norma always had presents and a tree at school, but Melissa hadn't *lived* with them. She watched us set up the tree but wasn't really interested until we turned the lights on. Then she learned the sign for "lights" in record time. We use the miniature lights and spent the holiday weeks trying to find and replace bulbs. Melissa would be fascinated by a light. It would come out in her hand, she would get disgusted when it didn't still light up, and she'd toss it away. We would see the lights off and scramble under the tree, trying to find the missing bulb. Years ago I gave up on fancy present wrappings, and I just use the stick-on bows. Searching for Melissa one afternoon, I found her sitting under the tree—festooned with sticky bows. She loved Christmas morning when we opened presents. She didn't care about the presents, just the opening.

In April we took Melissa to visit her audiologist. The doctor tested Melissa and started grinning. "I don't believe this!" he said. When the testing was over the doctor explained, "I've never seen her respond like she did today! Her right ear has a good amount of hearing." The doctor ordered new over-the-ear aids instead of the bulky body aids.

Melissa went to summer camp, and when she saw me ironing and packing her clothes, she suddenly got scared. We told her what was going on but weren't sure how much she understood.

We drove her to camp but got lost on the way and arrived three hours late. As we were going up the last stretch of road we met the camp bus—stuck. Dennis got out to talk to the director, who promptly started signing to Dennis. (We use the equivalent of baby talk with Melissa, and it hardly prepares us to sign with a fluent deaf adult.) We were all laughing at Daddy's communication problem when I got out to explain to the people in the car behind me and ran into the same problem.

I had expected to get lots of rest the week Melissa was gone, and lots of sleep. Instead, we spent the week asking, "When's she coming home?"

Melissa rode the bus home from camp, and when we went to pick her up the school nurse reported, "She's had a great week. You must send her back next summer." Melissa saw her daddy and flew. She ran to him, threw her arms around his neck, wrapped those bony legs around his waist, and then twisted her feet so she was locked on. She had a terrific week but was taking no chances on his getting away.

Melissa was to celebrate her birthday, and we went to a local office that helps the deaf so that we could order some signing books. The lady who could speak was using the phone, and she told me to go to the man at the other desk.

"Hello!" he signed.

"Hi!" I signed back. Then I attempted in my limited "Melissa sign" to explain, "Want books, my daughter." The poor man thought he was communicating with a retarded deaf adult and he answered me in sign very slowly, very simply.

As we struggled through our communications gap, I was beginning to wonder if I'd ever get the books ordered. Then Melissa wandered away and I yelled, "Melissa, come here!"

The startled man turned to me and said, "You can talk!"

"So can you!" I replied, equally startled.

We sent out invitations to Norma, the Cardozas, Grandma Mary, and Scotty (from Melissa's school): "We're having a joint celebration for Melissa's tenth birthday and our first year with her."

I decorated a cake with the sign for "I love you," and we decorated the kitchen with blue balloons. Dennis and I couldn't help but compare this year's birthday child with last year's. Melissa looked beautiful. She was much more alert, more grown up, and she knew it was *her* day.

As each guest arrived, Melissa would take *her* present and

stack it on the table; she played pin-the-tail on Mickey Mouse; and we all signed and sang "Happy Birthday." Melissa opened each present and was more interested in the contents than the wrappings. Scotty's mother embroidered a shirt with a hand signing "I love you," and it was Melissa's favorite gift.

In Melissa's scrapbook there's a picture from that party, and it's my very favorite of her: Norma is trying to get Melissa to blow out the ten candles, and Melissa looks bright, alert, and beautiful. The once-stubbly hair is lustrous and hangs past her shoulders, and she's wearing a sundress I made and her first pair of sandals.

Melissa had open-heart surgery when she was younger, and we were due to visit the cardiologist. In September, she had a bad ear infection and was put on penicillin.

She was in a lot of pain one night and ran a high fever, so we were up most of the night. She slept late the next morning, and when she undressed for her bath she was covered with a fine rash. My immediate thought was, *That looks just like the rash Robby had from penicillin!* I quickly dressed her and took her to the doctor. While we were waiting, the rash turned from the fine rash to thick welts all over her body. She was promptly given medication to stop the severe reaction, and no more penicillin for Melissa.

While she was itching from the horrid welts, even more frightening things were happening internally, and that afternoon she had three choking episodes. I was a basket case.

I ran bath water for Melissa, hoping that the water would help her feel more comfortable. I left the bathroom to check on one of the other kids, and when I returned there was Melissa: flat on her back, arms and legs straight at her sides, her eyes rolled back.

Oh, my God! *How will I tell Dennis, and the kids, and Norma, and her social worker, and....*

Then I saw her chest slowly rising. Melissa was exhausted, stretched out in the shallow water, and was entranced, watching a drop of water slowly drip from the faucet as ten years quickly dropped from me.

When she was well I took her to the cardiologist, and he ran an electrocardiogram (EKG) and chest X ray. Two doctors gave her a thorough exam, and one of them told me, "I no longer consider her a cardiac patient. If you ever have any questions, call me, but there's no need to bring her back."

There have been some really rough times with Melissa; some frightening times; and some precious times. One of the special moments was with Melissa and a hawk.

The ranger from a local nature center brought some birds to visit Melissa's school. There was an owl, a dove, and a hawk. Melissa has always been terrified of pets, and with all of our allergies there are no pets in our home.

Melissa wanted the owl to sit on her finger—until it showed off its enormous wingspread and scared her. She wanted nothing to do with the gentle little dove but was intrigued by the hawk.

The ranger was explaining the nature center and told the children in sign, "Hawks bite and have sharp talons, and that's why we always use these thick leather gloves."

We were so busy listening to the ranger that we'd ignored Melissa. And the hawk. Melissa was closely inspecting the hawk—very closely. Her eye was practically on the bird's talon as she checked it out. She would lift the wing and poke the tail feathers, and the hawk stood patiently through this indignity and looked haughtily down his beak at Melissa. Some extra sense seemed to have told that "wild" bird that this little girl was special and meant him no harm.

In her group home, Melissa was completely taken care of. I have neither the time nor the inclination to do that, and I was determined to help Melissa develop as much independence as possible.

That very first morning when she lifted her legs for me to undress her, I replied, "No way, kid! Here's your clothes. You put them on." And I left the room. I returned a few minutes later and found Melissa playing with her hands. I behaved very dramatically, yelled, and made faces. "No! No! It's time to get dressed!" And I left the room again.

When I returned, Melissa had one sock on and was unraveling the other. More theatrics. This routine went on for months until I could finally tell her to get dressed, leave the room, and she'd follow through on her own.

For a year Melissa mostly just existed here. I cooked and did the dishes and washed the clothes. She didn't notice any of it. Then one day Melissa realized that her dirty clothes went in the hamper, not back in her drawer.

We were excited and pleased with that measure of progress. Then she discovered that her clothes went in the washer and dryer, and she started dragging me to the garage to get me to unload the dryer and bring in her clean clothes. She'd sort out her own clothes and put them away.

With disgust, Melissa noticed when I was behind in my work. She stomped out to the garage, got the clothes basket, and brought the clothes inside. Then she folded all the clothes and put them away where they belonged.

"Thank you, Melissa." I would say. "You're such a good helper, and I'm so proud of you."

When she was asleep, I stealthily went around the house and collected all the clothes she had so neatly put away. None of them had been washed yet.

Melissa has taken over many of the laundry chores. I see this assumed skill as an indicator of the total progress she's made in independence, thinking skills, and responsibility.

When she comes home from school, she gets all the laundry out of the dryer and drags the basket in. She dumps out the clothes, gets all of hers, and puts them away. I fold up the other clothes and put them in stacks, and she puts them away: towels in the linen closet, each child's clothes in the proper room, dish towels in the kitchen. She'll even sign "please" if she's afraid I won't let her help (wish the other kids were that concerned). I've always prided myself on keeping a neat house, closets included. But now there's a little girl who's so proud of her new accomplishments, and that's more important than picture-perfect closets.

I recently returned from a long afternoon meeting, and I had a few harsh words for the kids and the chores they'd neglected. I went into my bedroom and found that all the laundry had been put away. Sheepishly, I went out to the kids. "I'm sorry," I told them. "Thanks for putting away the laundry."

Five voices yelled out, "It wasn't me!"

I went into Melissa's room, took her to the closet, closed my eyes to the messy pile of towels, and sincerely thanked her. Maybe next month we can work on neatness.

There have been many times since Melissa joined our family that I've asked myself and God, *Can I really handle this? Can I handle this in ten years or twenty? What is her future going to be?*

Over and over I get the same message, *One day at a time.* In the early days, when I was constantly exhausted from lack of sleep, I'd ask, *Can I even make it through another night? Will we have to give up and send her back?*

In my journal I'd written, "WHAT IF WE'RE HER ONLY CHANCE?" With that in mind and another prayer for strength, I'd vow to give it another day. Then another. Until I finally stopped asking the question.

Melissa has been a university course for us all. She's not only tested our faith, but she's also stretched it. We expected to give. We receive. We expected to teach. We learn.

Melissa doesn't feed our egos with lengthy compliments

and platitudes. She doesn't express any gratitude for being part of our family. She plays beside the kids, not with them. Through her, we're learning that true love cares more about the giving than the receiving.

With most children we expect routine, measurable progress. It's taken for granted, assumed. But Melissa follows no progress chart. We can make no assumptions. One of the blessings God gives us is a constant awareness of the real miracle involved in each minute step of progress, each new lesson learned, each folded towel. They're not assumptions, they're treasures. Where others see only the commonplace, *we see miracles.*

We're all learning to love and accept Melissa in the same way that God loves and accepts us, just as we are, with all our blemishes and shortcomings.

And the greatest of these is love.
1 Corinthians 13:13

9

Master Designer

NEEDLES AND THREAD. Darning. Feather stitch. Thorn stitch. Chain stitch. Such a variety of stitches has gone into this piece of needlework, and the tapestry of my life.

Feather Stitch

Momma Eagle has a warm, cozy nest prepared for her babies, but as they get bigger they have to learn to fly or they'll die. Momma Eagle knows this, but the babies don't. Those babies take one long look d-o-w-n, and they're convinced that they'd much rather stay in their soft, cozy—safe—nest.

Then Momma Eagle starts moving out the soft leaves, the downy feathers. The babes sit down, yell "Ouch!" and finally decide to give flying a try.

Some days my mother's heart breaks as I nudge Becky to master another skill, encourage Melissa to set the table or dress herself. They look at me with questioning eyes: "Does she really love me?"

And I picture old Momma Eagle as she removes the downy softness, nudges her timid eaglets out of the nest, then swoops to catch them on her majestic wingspread. I'm sure those babies look at her with questioning eyes as they plummet rapidly downward, and I wonder,

Do Momma Eagles cry, too?

Thorn Stitch

Stares and glares. People who don't understand and think we have some sort of "cause." Being disowned by relatives, dropped by friends.

But then my Lord knows all about thorns, and He lovingly wraps me in His arms, holds me tight, gives me a heavenly cuddle. Heals.

Chain Stitch

Chains interlocked. Circles interwoven. God took the pain of those early years with our first three children and gave us healing, then used the experiences that He'd entrusted to us as preparation for the next three children. Slow by our standards. Perfect by God's. His cycle of healing.

Just as the chain is made up of separate loops forming one chain, so the Lord has taken eight very separate people, gathered them here, and made a family.

A single strand of thread is weak, easily broken. But when many are interwoven, interlocked into the fabric, there's strength. As our lives become more interwoven with God, and each other, there's strength. Just as this material is made of interwoven strands, so God's love is the thread that holds us together.

Darning

Lord, some days I'm so weary that I seem to meet myself coming and going just trying to keep up with each month's twenty or thirty doctor and therapy appointments. If I hear one more child plead, "But I hafta have new shoes," or if I have to wipe up one more glass of milk, I'll cry out, "What am I doing here?"

Then You send Benji running to me—on legs they said would never run. He throws those beautiful brown arms around my neck, gives me a big, wet kiss, and says, "I wuv you, Mommy," and I know what I'm doing here.

> I'm something I'm not,
> Doing something I can't,
> But I can do all things through
> Christ Who strengthens me.

I sing and pray that little chorus as I drive to therapy appointments and baseball practices, and as I walk the halls at night. And I'm constantly reminded of who I really am, what my capabilities and limits really are, and where my strength really comes from.

Needles

Thoughtless words spoken in front of the children:
"Which ones are your *real* children?"
"Can you really love an adopted child like *your own?*"
"Ones like him must be easier to get."
"Babysitting?"
"Who will they date when they're older?"
"Will they always have to live with you?"
"Can she understand what I am saying?"
"Cripple!"
"Nigger!"

Stitches. Threads that were singed; never burned. That hurt; never broke. *And Lord, You've been there with us. Caring that children walk and talk. Caring about blue windbreakers and white T-shirts. Teaching the children to love You, their Heavenly Father, through Dennis, their earthly father. Walking dark halls with me on sleepless, weary nights.*

Stitch after stitch, the Master Designer has let us hold miracles, know His presence, and see His love in action—a love that ignores color lines and birth lines.

As I've taken these multicolored threads and made a picture, so God has taken multihued people,

> "Red & yellow, black & white,
> they're at Wheeler's house
> tonight,"
>
> and woven us into a family.

Stitch after stitch,
we've gone through testings,
seen Your love.
Been down to the pits...
> *and touched the stars.*

Stitch after stitch,
You've patiently and lovingly
turned our sorrows into joys,
our tragedy into triumph,
our pain into victory...
> *our braces into blessings.*